We hope you enjoy this book. Please return or renew it by the due date.

You can renew it at www.norfolk.gov.uk/libraries or by using our free library app.

Otherwise you can phone 0344 800 8020 - please have your library card and PIN ready.

You can sign up for email reminders too.

The Canal Pioneers

The Canal Pioneers

Canal Construction from 2,500 BC
to the Early 20th Century

Anthony Burton

PEN & SWORD
TRANSPORT

First published in Great Britain in 2017 by
Pen & Sword Transport
an imprint of
Pen & Sword Books Ltd
47 Church Street
Barnsley
South Yorkshire
S70 2AS

ISBN 978 1 47386 049 0

A CIP catalogue record for this book is available from the British Library

Typeset in Ehrhardt by
Mac Style Ltd, Bridlington, East Yorkshire
Printed and bound in China by Imago Publishing Ltd

Pen & Sword Books Ltd incorporates the imprints of Pen & Sword
Archaeology, Atlas, Aviation, Battleground, Discovery, Family History,
History, Maritime, Military, Naval, Politics, Railways, Select, Transport, True
Crime, and Fiction, Frontline Books, Leo Cooper, Praetorian Press, Seaforth
Publishing and Wharncliffe.

For a complete list of Pen & Sword titles please contact
PEN & SWORD BOOKS LIMITED
47 Church Street, Barnsley, South Yorkshire, S70 2AS England
E-mail: enquiries@pen-and-sword.co.uk
Website: www.pen-and-sword.co.uk

Contents

Introduction

My interest in canals began more than half a century ago. My wife and I had taken a couple of canoeing holidays: the first down the Thames had been uneventful, but the second on the Wye ended disastrously when we holed the boat going down rapids and sank with all hands. We decided to try something different and less dampening in every sense. Friends had recently rented a boat on the Llangollen Canal, showed us the photos and we booked to do the same the next year. It was an instant love affair and, like everyone who travels that way for the first time, we were overwhelmed by the wonderful experience of crossing the spectacular Pontcysyllte aqueduct. I developed an interest in the people who had built the system and had created such engineering marvels.

Some years afterwards I left a career in publishing to strike out on my own as a freelance writer. I intended to be a humourist and my first book did well, appearing in hardback and paperback in Britain and America and being translated into other languages: I still have the to me incomprehensible Japanese edition on a shelf. My second foray into humour sank as completely as our canoe on the Wye. It was then that my agent, Murray Pollinger, asked a vital question: 'What is the book you have read recently that you would most like to have written yourself?' I didn't have to think: *The Railway Navvies* by Terry Coleman. Was there anything similar I could produce? And that is how I came to write *The Canal Builders*, still in print some forty years later and now in its fifth edition.

Since that book appeared I have continued to write about canals, and broadened the scope of my canal travels. I have travelled canals in continental Europe and seen something of waterways in North America and Asia. Up to now I had concentrated on British waterways, but I was realising that they are only a part of a much larger story. So this book is, in a way, a continuation of the work that began with *The Canal Builders* but in an international framework. It does not pretend to be a comprehensive account of canals around the world. It is specifically about canal construction and only deals with boats and cargo carrying to the extent that they affected the way in which engineers chose to build canals. Nor does it look at all canals everywhere. I have selected canals from around the world that provide the best examples of trends and developments through the years.

Research has been fascinating and I have received a lot of help from canal enthusiasts in different countries, especially from canal societies and associations in America and Ireland. And, of course, I have only been able to do this work because of other historians working long before I took up pen or tapped a keyboard. In particular I acknowledge my debt to two writers, L.T.C. Rolt and Charles Hadfield. Tom Rolt was especially kind when I started writing about this subject. I not only benefited from reading Charles Hadfield's many books but also got to know him as a friend in later years – and had an amicable battle about the relative merits of William Jessop and Thomas Telford. Both these authors have added immensely to everyone's knowledge of canals and their history. I could not have written this book on the magnificent canal pioneers without their equally splendid pioneering efforts.

Chapter 1

Beginnings: The Ancient World

No one knows when people developed boats for transport, but it must have been obvious from observation that large wooden objects floated down rivers with ease: objects that would have been extremely difficult to haul overland. It was only in the eighteenth century that anyone tried to measure the difference between land carriage and water carriage, with experiments that showed that if you put a pack on a horse's back it could carry up to 1/8th of a tonne and pulling a cart on a well-made road, a rarity at the time, it could manage a maximum of 2 tonnes. But harness it to haul a boat along a river and it could shift a more impressive 30 tonnes and, on the still waters of a canal, the load was increased to 50 tonnes. Tomb engravings show that the ancient Egyptians had boats at least as early as 2500 BC.

Rivers were clearly the most efficient means of moving heavy goods from one place to another and their importance was recognised: in medieval Britain, for example, the Severn was known as 'The King's Highway of Severn'. Navigable rivers were invaluable, which is why great inland cities grew up along their banks. But they have problems. The ideal transport route would be a river that flowed smoothly and evenly in a straight line from place to place. Few rivers match that ideal. They meander across the countryside; sometimes they dash furiously through rapids and falls; in other places they widen out with shallows and shoals. And there may be some very bulky commodity that needed to be transported, but which was not found anywhere near a navigable river. A navigable canal avoids these problems, but it requires considerable technical, surveying and engineering skills to construct. In Britain we think of canals as being a product of the Industrial Revolution of the eighteenth century, but canals were being constructed thousands of years earlier. The story of canals, however, is not one of smooth, continuous development. It is rather more complex than that.

As with the development of boats, the earliest history of canal construction may be lost or obscure, but we know that the Egyptians began constructing canals during the 6th Dynasty under the Pharaoh Pepi I, who ruled from 2332–2283 BC. Egypt had a major transport problem. The pharaohs wanted to build pyramids, but the sites were seldom conveniently close to stone quarries, so they needed an efficient system for moving massive blocks of stone. An account has survived in the tomb of Weni or Uni the Elder, a general in the Pharaoh's army, telling us that he was ordered to construct five canals, which were completed in one year, and to build three barges and four towboats of acacia wood. They were to move granite blocks for the pyramid Merenre. The canals were to be used first to bring stone to the Nile and then also to improve navigation on the river. The Nile has a

Rivers had been the most efficient means of transporting goods since ancient times, and the prime importance of the Severn in England led to it being referred to as 'The King's Highway of Severn'. This busy scene at the confluence of the Severn and the Avon at Tewkesbury in the eighteenth century, with boats of many different types, goes a long way to explain how the name arose. The principal sailing barge of the area was the Severn trow, which in its earlier form was square rigged like the vessels shown here. (*Tewkesbury Town Council*)

series of cataracts, and at the first of these Weni constructed a bypass canal. This had to be cut through the solid rock and although it was comparatively short, just 90m long, it was wide and deep enough, 10m by 9m, to take the largest vessels on the river.

The most ambitious scheme was for a canal to link the Nile with the Red Sea, but information is scant. It was probably built at some time before 1000 BC, but whether it was ever completed at that time is doubtful and it eventually fell into disuse. The scheme was revised when construction began under the Pharaoh Neko or Nekhau. It linked the river to the Bitter Lakes, north of the Red Sea, and was eventually completed under the Persian ruler Darius I. For once, we have a reasonably full account by the Greek historian Herodotus. The quotation comes from Macauley's translation of Herodotus:

'The length of this is a voyage of four days, and in breadth was so dug that two triremes could go side by side driven by oars; and the water is brought in from the Nile. The channel is conducted a little above the city of Bubastis [an ancient city in the Nile Delta approximately 80km north east of Cairo] by Patumos the Arabian city and runs into the Erythraian Sea [Red Sea] and it is dug first along those parts of the plain of Egypt which lie towards Arabia, just above which run the mountains which extend opposite Memphis, where are the stone quarries – along the base of these mountains the channel is conducted from West to East for a great way; and after that it is directed towards a break in the hills and tends from these mountains towards the noon-day and South Wind to the Arabian gulf. Now in the place where the journey is least and shortest from the Northern to the Southern Sea (which is also called Erythraian), that is from Mount Casion, which is the boundary between Egypt and Syria, the distance is exactly a thousand furlongs to the Arabian gulf; but the channel is much longer, since it is more winding; and in the reign of Necos there perished while digging it twelve myriads of the Egyptians. Now Necos ceased in the midst of his digging, because the utterance of an Oracle impeded him, which was to the effect that he was working for the barbarian; and the Egyptians call all men barbarians who do not agree with them in speech.'

Not the most exciting account of canal construction ever written, but it tells us a lot. It is obvious that the route was carefully chosen to maintain a level, suggesting considerable surveying skills. This is not surprising, given that these were the people who managed the complex geometry of pyramid construction. It also indicates that a vast labour force was involved. That is one advantage of being a pharaoh: you can command as many men as you need to do a job. The death toll is extraordinary, even if Herodotus was exaggerating: a myriad is 10,000 so he is telling us that 120,000 died building the canal. When completed the canal was a fine waterway, roughly 50m wide and 100km long. It was opened c.500 BC and monuments were erected lauding the work. Not too surprisingly, Darius claimed all the glory, described as 'king of kings, king of the countries of all languages, king of the wide and far-off earth' and the inscription ends 'This stream was dug as I have ordered.'

We have few details about the working of the canal. We do know that in the third century BC there was considerable reconstruction and a new device was added by Ptolemy Philadelphus, described by a contemporary, Diodorus Siculus, as 'an ingenious kind of lock. This he opened, whenever he wished to pass through, and quickly closed again, a contrivance whose usage proved to be highly successful.' That he had to get through as quickly as possible means that it could not have been the sort of lock with which we are familiar, but one with a single gate, holding back water at a higher level that would allow a flood of water to pass through when it was opened. We shall meet this device later when we look at developments in China and at later river improvements in Europe. The canal was not a huge success, largely because of the amount of silt carried down from the Nile, and it fell into disuse. Watery connection between the Mediterranean and the Red Sea was only re-established with the construction of the Suez Canal in the nineteenth century.

During the wars between Persia and Greece in the fifth century BC, Xerxes avoided taking his ships round the long peninsula that ends at Mount Athos and ordered a canal to be cut across the narrow neck of land where it joined the mainland. It was to be 4km long and Herodotus describes how it was dug, the first of its kind in written records:

Few of the earliest canals built in the ancient world have survived in recognisable form, either in physical remains or in pictures. One early scheme planned to cut through the narrow Corinth Isthmus in the south of Greece. The various schemes proved impossible given the available technology. Seeing the canal today, carved deep through solid rock, one can understand why it only finally opened in 1893. (*Alfien Crispin*)

'When the trench reached a certain depth, the labourers at the bottom carried on with the digging and passed the soil up to others above them, who stood on ladders and passed it on to another lot, still higher up, until it reached the men at the top, who carried it away and dumped it. Most of the people engaged in the work made the cutting the same width at the top as it was intended to be at the bottom, with the inevitable result that the sides kept falling in, and so doubled their labour. Indeed they all made this mistake except the Phoenicians, who in this – as in all other practical matters – gave a signal example of their skill. They, in the section allotted to them, took out a trench double the width prescribed for the actual finished canal, and by digging at a slope gradually contracted it as they got further down, until at the bottom their section was the same width as the rest.'

There was an even more obvious site for a useful canal in the Isthmus of Corinth that separates the Peloponnese from the Greek mainland. The first attempt was made in the seventh century BC by Periander, but he soon abandoned the idea of a canal in favour of a portage system overland for his ships. Known as the Diolkos, it consisted of a paved road, with grooves cut to take standard-sized wagons, an idea that re-emerged in Europe some 2,000 years later. There are still traces of this ancient way alongside the modern canal. The canal idea was revised under Demetrius Poliorcetes about 300 BC, but his surveyors told him, incorrectly as it turned out, that there was a difference in sea levels between the two ends, and they feared flooding. He abandoned the idea. The whole scheme was shelved until the Romans revived it. After several false starts, work began under Nero in AD 67. The Emperor cut the first sod himself, then handed over the work to thousands of Jewish slaves, imprisoned during the recent wars. They dug trenches at either end, and in the central ridge they dug exploratory shafts to test the nature of the rock. When Nero died the attempt died with him. Construction of a ship canal only started again in 1881 and if the ancients could have seen the result, they would have realised the impossibility of what they had taken on: in the centre, it carves through solid rock and the almost vertical walls rise to a height of 90m. Such a task would have defeated even the skills of Roman engineers.

In the description of the canal near Mount Athos, Herodotus referred to the skills of the Phoenicians. They were, in fact, masters of canal construction, but their works were built for water supply, not for navigation. Nevertheless, they used advanced technology that could have been adapted for any canal work. One of the most remarkable achievements was a canal to bring water from the Greater Zab to Sennacherib's capital city Nineveh in 691 BC. It was 50 miles long and paved with stone throughout its course and as wide as a main road. Stone was brought from quarries in the hills and an estimated two million limestone blocks were shifted. One reason for paving the bed of the canal was to use it as a roadway during the construction period. A weir was built across the river to divert water into the canal, overlooked by massive figures of the king himself and various gods, together with an inscription recounting that the whole work was completed in one year and three months.

The most impressive single feature was a 300m long stone aqueduct carried on five corbelled arches that crossed the valley near Nineveh. Corbelled arches are constructed by

The Romans are famous for their skills as civil engineers, especially for building roads. They were equally competent in constructing canals, primarily for either irrigation or water supply. Some of these waterways were also used for transport. That they could have built imposing canals is obvious from what they did construct, of which the aqueduct over the River Gard, the Pont du Gard, is an outstanding example. It is now classified as a UNESCO World Heritage site. (*Wolfgang Staudt*)

building up a structure of slightly overlapping stones, so that the two sides gradually get close enough together until they can be bridged by a capping stone. It was the Romans who made spectacular use of true arches, in which the arch is built over a wooden former, also known as centring. This is an arch constructed of timber, on top of which the stones can be laid. Once the keystone is in place, holding the stones firmly together, the wooden structure can safely be removed. They used the arches in building even more immense aqueducts for water supply, of which the most famous is the Pont du Gard near Nîmes.

Most of the 50km of the aqueduct lies underground, but the engineers had, at some point, to cross the River Gardon. They selected a point where the river narrows between rocky ledges that provided solid foundations for the structure. They built six arches, with massive piers each 6m thick and rising to a height of 22m. This created a solid bridge 142m long, on which a row of 11 smaller arches was constructed, extending the length of the aqueduct to 242m. A third layer of even smaller arches, with piers just 3m thick and 7m high, completed the structure that now extended to 275m. Originally there were forty-seven arches in the top layer, but today only thirty-five remain. To build such a structure at all shows great daring and confidence – but it also demanded great accuracy. The water in the aqueduct flowed by gravity along a very gentle slope of just 1 in 3,000; the difference in height between the two ends of the structure is a paltry 2½cm, small but sufficient to keep the water flowing steadily.

The Romans had clearly developed sophisticated surveying techniques – the straightness of their main roads is legendary. Their two principal instruments were the groma and the chorobates. The groma consisted of a vertical rod, some 2m high, with a swivelling crosspiece, with plumb lines suspended from the ends. It lined up the instrument with poles held at a distance by an assistant. The chorobates was rather more complex. It consisted of a rod, as much as 6m long, supported at either end by identical legs. These were joined to the rod by diagonal struts, marked with vertical lines. When plumb lines hung from the rod above, the struts were perfectly in line with the markings, then the rod was level and could be used as a reference point. When the plumb lines would wave about in the wind, the surveyors could use a water trough on top of the rod to obtain a level. However, Jean-Pierre Adam carried out experiments with a chorobates and the best accuracy he could get was 1.16 per cent – nowhere near the accuracy that we find in the actual aqueduct. N.A.F. Smith, in an article in the *Transactions of the Newcomen Society (Vol.62)*, suggests that a different device might have been used, an A-frame level called a libella.

At the Pont du Gard the actual construction was helped by cranes and block and tackle arrangements. The stones were carefully cut and inscribed with a code of letters and numbers, indicating where they would be placed in the structure, marks that are still visible today. One of the more remarkable features of the aqueduct is that no mortar was used: it relied entirely on the accuracy of the mason to provide perfectly shaped blocks that would fit snugly together. There was never any intention of using this system for transport, but as with the Phoenicians the technology could have been used to build navigable canals.

When it came to building canals for land drainage, it is suggested that they would also have been used for boats, possibly even in Roman Britain. One of these drainage systems is the Car Dyke in Lincolnshire, which is certainly post-Iron Age and probably Roman. The section from the River Witham to the River Slea was certainly navigable and there is inconclusive evidence that suggests it was used by boats. No such doubts exist about the Foss Dyke that runs from the Trent, near Torksey, for just over 11 miles to Lincoln and is still navigable today. Bizarrely it ended its working days of cargo carrying in the ownership of the London & North Eastern Railway. What would the Roman engineers have made of that?

Canals of various kinds were constructed over a long period in the ancient world throughout Europe and the Middle East and there were some remarkable achievements. However, nothing built in this period can compare with what was happening across the world in China.

The story begins with a war, when in about 215 BC the Emperor sent troops to conquer the province of Yüeh. According to a document written some time after the event, a fighting force was sent by boat to conquer the region and, at the same time, an order was made for a canal to be cut to supply them with grain during the campaign. It became known as the Ling Chhü or Magic Canal and the engineer was Shi Lu. Early texts refer to the canal but according to Joseph Needham, the author of the most authoritative English language work covering Chinese canal history, *Science and Society in China, Vol.4,* 1971, the most complete account comes from a work of 1178, which he quotes in a lengthy translation, part of which appears below. The canal was built to link two rivers: the Hsiang that flows north towards the Yangtze and the Li flowing south. Construction involved building up a stone barrier that was known as a 'spade-like snout' in the middle of the Hsiang to divide its waters, so that one part could be diverted into the canal. From there the canal entered an embanked section and then followed a contour round the hills for a total of about 20 miles. This section has a natural flow and is provided with numerous spillways to avoid flooding. The most intriguing part of the account describes what it was like to travel the canal:

> 'In the canal there are 36 lock gates. As each vessel enters one of these lock gates, (the people) immediately restore it to its closed position and wait while water accumulates (within the lock) so that by this means the ship gradually progresses.'

In such a way they are able to follow the mountainside and move upwards.

> 'On the descent, it is like water flowing down the stepped groove of a roof, and thus there is communication for the boats between north and south. I myself have seen (I am happy to say) the historic traces of the work of Lu.'

The most complex canal system devised in the ancient world was the Grand Canal of China, the oldest parts of which date back to the sixth century BC. It stretched for more than 1,000km and has survived, although much changed over the years, to the present day. One of the officials with the Macartney Mission to China of 1793 was a draughtsman, William Alexander, who sketched the canal. His drawings appeared as engravings in a book, *Costume of China*, published in 1805. This illustration shows a lifting bridge across the canal. The team of working men were supplied with the shelter to the right of the bridge.

There can be little doubt that what is being described is some form of pound lock, but it is unknown whether such locks were there from the start of work or were later additions. Where the canal met the Li it continued as a lateral canal beside the river. From all the evidence, Needham concludes that the locks date from the tenth or eleventh century. With its construction, China possessed a continuous line of waterways stretching for more than 1,200 miles and it remains in use.

The best-known ancient canal in China is the Grand Canal. It was not devised as a single waterway but grew out of several schemes spread over many centuries. It had its origins not so much in transport as irrigation. It began with the construction of the Hung Kou, translated as the Wild Geese Canal, which linked the Yellow River with the Huai River. The difference in levels between the two river systems was so small that vessels could use it without needing any sluice or lock. It is usually dated to about the late sixth century BC. The next section was Han Kuo, built as a military canal in the fifth century BC to join the Huai to the Yangtze. In its original form it appears to have been a very meandering waterway that was later modernised. The canal was extended over the centuries and in the sixth century AD new sections were supplied with flash locks: single gates that closed off an upper section of the canal from the lower, but when opened allowed vessels to ride down

This is another of Alexander's illustrations of the Grand Canal. Originally the differences in levels between different sections of the canal were negotiated through locks, but in later years these were replaced by slipways. The vessel is being hauled by ropes to the top of the slipway by two gangs of men working capstans. The European standing in the bows is presumably a Mission official.

on the current. Where the differences in levels were too great for a flash lock, slipways were built, along which vessels could be winched up or down. One of the most impressive achievements came when problems occurred in supplying water to the summit level of the canal, 138ft above the mean level of the Yangtze. This was solved in the early fifteenth century, a century after the through route had been completed, with the construction of a vast dam on the Kuang River to create a reservoir. Just as the pharaohs had been able to call up an army of workers for huge construction projects, so the same system could be used in Imperial China. The workforce numbered 165,000 men and they completed the task in just 200 days.

The Grand Canal was a mixture of river navigations and artificial waterways, and eventually extended for 1,035 miles from Beijing to Hangzhou. It was an immense achievement, but was unknown to Europeans and when they did eventually reach China the pound locks appear to have disappeared, to be replaced by slipways and flash locks. An illustration by William Alexander of the British Embassy shows the canal in c.1800. Where we would expect to see a lock, the boat is about to be lowered on rollers down a slipway. So, in spite of the achievements and engineering ability of the Chinese, the works had virtually no effect on developments in Europe. Everything would have to be invented all over again.

Chapter 2

Navigation Improvements

Following the collapse of the Roman Empire and the decline of the great Mediterranean civilisations, Europe entered a period known as the Dark Ages. Rivers continued to be used for transport, but little was done to improve them for many centuries. By the medieval period a new type of obstacle impeded navigation. In Britain, the eleventh-century *Domesday Book* recorded more than 10,000 mills in England. These were water mills, many of which ensured a steady supply of water to turn their wheels by building weirs. These created a good head of water upstream of the dam, which could then be diverted down an artificial channel to the mill. They also effectively blocked the river as far as transport was concerned.

One of the most detailed accounts of travel on a long river was supplied by John Taylor, waterman and poet. His book *The Description of Thames and Isis* (1632) sets out to tell the reader, in verse, exactly what he intends to do:

The River Thames at Windsor Castle in the seventeenth century. The early Thames sailing barges have square bows and sterns, not unlike an enlarged version of a modern punt. The ones with sails set clearly have a following wind, whereas barges going in the opposite direction are either being rowed or, having dropped their sails, are being towed. A team of horses can be seen on the spit of land that forms one side of a cutting leading down to the water mill. (*Her Majesty the Queen*)

'But I (from Oxford) down to Staines will slide,
And tell the rivers wrongs which I espied.'

And foremost among those wrongs were the weirs built by millers:

Haules Weare doth almost cross the river all,
Making the passage straight and very small,
How can that man be counted a good liver
That for his private use will stop a river?'

To overcome such obstacles, the Thames had, by this time, a series of flash locks. The flash lock would be built into a gap in the weir. This consisted of two baulks of timber: one, usually of elm, fixed firmly to the riverbed; the other above the water was moveable. The two beams were joined by vertical posts called rimers, in between which were wooden paddles with long handles. When a boat approached, the paddles were raised, allowing water to flow through so that the gate, with its rimers, could be swung out of the way. This released a flood of water, the flash, which a boat could ride downstream, and boats travelling upstream were winched up against the current. Using the flash locks was by

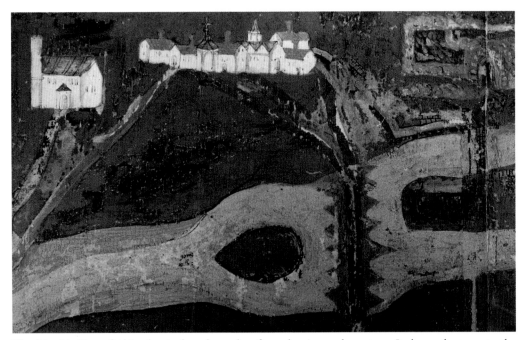

The Monk's Map of Abingdon is thought to date from the sixteenth century. It shows the town to the north of the bridge. To the right of that, the river divides: the northern branch has a flash lock that allows boats to pass when opened. (*Abingdon County Hall Museum*)

A typical flash lock from William Armstrong's nineteenth-century book *The Thames*. The illustration shows the lock keeper lifting one of the wooden paddles that are set within the vertical timber framework of the 'rimers'. Once the paddles have been removed, the gate can be swung open to allow a boat to pass down with the rush of water, or 'flash' that gives this type of early lock its name. (*Anthony Burton*)

no means straightforward and, as Taylor reported, there were always other problems to contend with:

> 'The Sutton locks are great impediments,
> The waters fall with such great violence,
> Thence downe to Cullam [Culham], streame runs quicke and quicker,
> Yet we rub'd twice a ground for want of liquor.'

At least he got down safely. In 1634 a passenger boat, with an estimated sixty men, women and children on board, overturned in the flash at Goring. They all drowned. The earliest reference to such a device on the Thames, known then by its alternative name of 'stanch' or 'staunch', is 1306. Surprisingly the last flash lock on the Thames was still in use at Eynsham until it was replaced in 1931.

The last flash lock on the Thames remained in place until well into the twentieth century at Eynsham on the river above Oxford. The gate has been opened and the photograph captures the rapid movement of the water. This was a comparatively small drop: with some of the large flash locks the flow would have been even stronger and accidents were common. Vessels moving downstream rode the flood while those going upstream were either manhandled up on small locks or winched up against the flow. (*Oxfordshire County Libraries*)

As in the ancient world, navigable canals in Holland had their origin in the complex system of dykes used to drain the low-lying lands. The outlets were generally controlled through sluice gates that became obstacles when the dykes were widened to take vessels. There were two options. The earliest solution was probably to unload the cargo and carry it round to load it back into another boat on the far side of the gate. Very early on, however, ramps were built to allow the boats themselves to be hauled between the two levels. The earliest use of ramps appears to date back to the Nieuwe Rijn canal built in 1148. A better solution was to build large sluices so that boats could actually pass through. All these devices were of the portcullis type, in which the gates were lifted vertically instead of being swung open. This system allowed boats to pass between the dykes and tidal rivers and estuaries when the levels were equal. It was at best a clumsy system as tidal waters and dykes only reached a level twice a day. An important variation first appeared at Vreeswilk near Utrecht, where the canal joined the Lek river. Records show that in 1378, two sluice gates were built close together, in effect creating a basin, in which vessels could wait until conditions were right for them to move out in either direction, from river to canal or vice versa. It was, in effect, a very large lock. One lock of this type, built near Bruges at the end

The alternative to the flash lock was the pound lock. As its name implies this is a lock in which the water is impounded between gates. Sluices, controlled by paddles, allow the water to pass in from the upper level of the waterway to fill the lock or to drain out at the lower level to empty it. This early illustration shows the device at its simplest. The two sets of gates are set directly into the river and are raised and lowered vertically, hence the name 'portcullis lock'. The diagram shows the lifting mechanism set at the top of the portcullis, with no indication of how the lock keeper was actually going to work it. (*Biblioteca Medicea-Laurenziana, Florence*)

The portcullis, or as it was also known, the guillotine lock, was rarely used on later canals. This example is a stop lock, separating the Stratford Canal from the Worcester & Birmingham at King's Norton Junction. The sketch in the previous illustration gave only the vaguest idea of how such a lock might be worked. Here it is much clearer. The gate is lifted by means of the windlass that can be seen to the right of the lock and is counterbalanced by weights that can be lowered by means of a chain running over the pulley to the right. (*Waterways Archive Gloucester*)

of the fourteenth century, had a chamber that measured 30m by 10½m. The idea was not, as we saw in the previous chapter, original. But China had been a closed society and by the time the first Europeans entered the country, the locks on the Grand Canal had been replaced by slipways. It was as if the Europeans had just reinvented the wheel.

The Dutch locks were not used to overcome differences in heights in the land – rarely a problem in Holland – but only to make up the difference between the constant levels of the canals and the ever-changing levels of the natural waterways. The next important development was the building of the Stecknitz Canal, between 1391 and 1398. This was a summit-level canal, in other words one that has a central section appreciably higher than the levels at either end. The River Stecknitz had already been made navigable from Lübeck to Lake Mölln, 21 miles to the south by conventional stanches. It was now proposed to continue the southern route as far as the Elbe. The River Delvenau met the Elbe at Lauenburg, but there was still a gap between that river and the lake that had to be filled by an artificial canal. It rose 5m from the lake in less than a kilometre, which involved constructing two locks, 10m long by 3½m beam, each capable of taking ten small boats. Beyond the locks, the canal ran for a further 5 miles in a cutting to reach the river.

Locks up to this time had virtually all been closed off with portcullis gates, which had to be laboriously raised to a considerable height to allow boats to pass underneath. There is uncertainty about who came up with a new design for lock gates that has remained the pattern for locks ever since, but there is no doubt about who first described and drew them. The Renaissance was a great age for polymaths, and none covered a wider range of subjects and interest than the now world-famous artist Leonardo da Vinci. He had arrived in Milan in 1482 and by 1498 had been appointed as state engineer with special responsibility for overseeing river navigations and canals. He constructed six new locks for the Naviglio Interno in Milan and in 1497 he set about improving the Martesana Canal. Work had begun on this as long ago as 1443 and da Vinci's task was to design a new lock just below the basin at San Marco. He sketched his idea in a notebook that was later bound with other da Vinci sketches as part of the massive *Codex Atlanticus* now held in a library at Milan. The drawing shows mitre gates. Instead of being raised vertically they are swung horizontally, meeting at an angle. The gates are both angled to point upstream, so that the force of water actually pushes them closer together to make a good watertight seal. Once water levels are equalised they are easily swung apart by means of balance beams. An almost identical sketch could easily have been made today on almost any canal in Britain.

The mitre gates didn't actually come into use in Britain until the sixteenth century. Navigation on the River Exe between Exeter and the sea was hampered by a structure that effectively closed off the river, the Countess Wear. Control of the Wear was in the hands of the people of Topsham, who had a thriving port and little interest in any changes that would allow ships to bypass them and head straight up to the city. But the citizens of Exeter had other ideas, and in 1564 they employed an engineer, John Trew, to design a

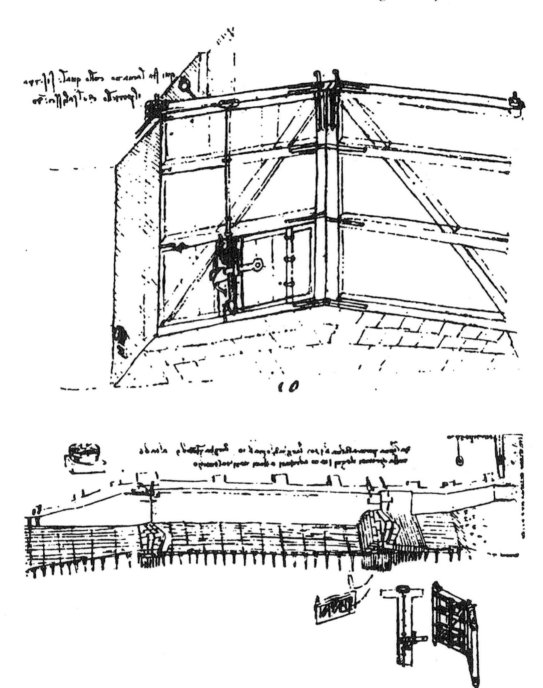

The portcullis was difficult to operate and created problems for high-masted vessels using the waterway. A better solution would obviously be conventional gates, but there would have been a tendency for them to be forced open by the pressure of water behind them. The solution was found by Leonardo da Vinci with his invention of the mitre gates. As the sketches show, the gates meet at an angle, with the 'vee' always pointing towards the higher level of water. As a result, instead of tending to push the gates apart, water pressure held them closer together. This is the system, invented in the fifteenth century, which is found in all modern canals. (*Biblioteca Ambrosiana, Milan*)

Work on improving navigation on the German rivers, Havel and Spree, took place in the sixteenth century. One of the first locks built was constructed at Brandenburg in 1548 and the work was completed in 1578 with the opening of a lock in Berlin. This sketch of the Brandenburg lock was reproduced in a German technical journal of 1908. Unlike modern locks, this was in effect a holding basin, designed on an octagonal plan with narrow openings at either end. The form of the lock gates is unknown. The diagram clearly shows the sides of the lock as being built up of timber piles.

canal. Very little is known about him apart from the fact that he was 'a gentleman from Glamorganshire'. It is a comparatively short canal, a mere 5 miles long, from a basin at Exeter to the point where it joins the estuary. A lock was built at the seaward end, very much in the manner of the Dutch holding locks. It was an immense affair, 189ft long and 23ft wide, closed at the upstream end with a pair of mitre gates. These had six sluices covered with paddles built into them to let the water in and out. The estuary end was closed by a single gate. The sides of the lock were lined with turf and although the original has long since been replaced, it is still known as Turf Lock and is overlooked by The Turf pub. The canal allowed large ships to reach the heart of Exeter and is officially known as the Exeter Ship Canal, but its importance dwindled as ships increased in size, soon reaching a point where larger vessels could no longer fit into the canal.

Many of the sixteenth-century canal locks built in Europe shared the Turf Lock's overall structure, being in effect holding basins that could take several vessels at any one time. One good example is the octagonal lock at Brandenburg, built between 1548 and 1550. In Britain, the first lock constructed with mitre gates at both ends was built as part of a

A similarly large lock was built on the Exeter Canal at much the same time as the Brandenburg lock. The route along the River Exe to the sea was blocked by the massive Countess Wear, so a canal was built to bypass it. Intended to take the largest ships of the day, it brought vessels right up to the edge of the city, where a large basin was constructed, together with a new customs house. This early photograph is excellent evidence that large sailing vessels could reach the dockside in Exeter. (*ISCA Collection*)

scheme for improving navigation on the River Lea at Waltham Abbey. There is a poetic account of the structure, published in 1590: *A Tale of Two Swannes* by William Vallan. This fanciful work finds two swans travelling up the river to see all the sights. It is worth quoting at some length, both as one of the earliest descriptions of an English river navigation, and also because it shows that this was still such a novelty that Vallan thought it worth explaining in some detail to his readers:

'Down all along through Waltham street they passe
And wonder at the ruines of the Abbey,
Late supprest, the walles, the walkes, the monuments,
And everie thing that there is to be seene.
Among them all a rare devise they see,
But newly made, a waterworke: the locke
Through which the boats of Ware doe passé with malt.
This locke contains two double doores of wood,

Within the same a Cesterne all of Plancke,
Which onely fils when boates come there to passe
By opening anie of these mightie doores with sleight
And strange devise…'

A lock, with a wooden chamber and double mitre gates, was clearly a great curiosity.

Canals spread across much of Europe in the sixteenth century. In what was then Flanders, now Belgium, a canal was built to join Brussels to Willebroek on the tidal River Rupel. The aim was to greatly shorten the distance that coastal vessels had to travel to reach Brussels. It was first approved by Philip the Good in 1483, but the city of Mechelen that was doing rather well out of taxation on vessels using the original river route, objected. The plans were shelved until 1550, when work began and the Mayor of Brussels, Jean de Locquenghien, cut the first sod. He also acted as director of the project with an assistant to help with the surveying and two resident engineers to supervise the day-to-day construction work. It was a canal built to a generous scale: 28km long, 30m wide and 2m deep, with locks constructed to take a dozen small coastal vessels. There were initially just four locks to overcome a fall of 10½m. One problem was the need to cross seven substantial streams along the way: all were diverted under the canal in wooden culverts, one of which leaked so badly it had to be replaced by a new one constructed of masonry. The most imposing engineering works was a cutting 3km long and up to 10m deep.

Among the most important early river navigations was the Aire & Calder. This view of the navigation at Leeds by J. Le Keux is dated 1715. It shows the sort of arrangements that were made. The sailing barge is approaching the lock that is set in a long artificial cutting. To the right of the cutting is the weir that allows water to flow freely, even when the lock is in use, unlike the primitive portcullis lock shown earlier. (*Leeds Central Library*)

The final section of the canal between the lowest of the locks and the river ran between two dykes, separating it from the low-lying marshy land to either side. Being linked directly to the river, this section of the canal was tidal. Soon after the canal opened in 1561 this reach caused trouble as silt was carried up from the river. In 1570 a tidal lock was built to cure the problem. This was a massive affair with three pairs of gates: one pair at the river end and two at the canal end. The inner pair were mounted above a low sill, the outer pair only reaching down to the level of the canal bed. It was a great success for almost everyone. Brussels became a busy inland port with several new canal basins. The losers were the citizens of Mechelen who, as feared, saw their tax revenue die away.

In Britain in the seventeenth and early eighteenth century, the emphasis was not so much on artificial canals as on improving existing river systems. In 1660 there were roughly 660 miles of navigable river in Britain. By 1720 that figure rose to 1,160 miles. Among the more ambitious schemes was that for the Aire & Calder Navigation. The Aire has a dramatic start in life at the foot of the limestone cliff of Malham Cove and then vanishes underground for a time before emerging in full flow in Airedale. This area was already noted for its thriving woollen industry, at this time still largely carried out in workers' own homes. The Calder rises high in the Pennines above the town of Todmorden and, like the Aire, runs through an area noted for its woollen industry. The two rivers unite at Castleford and beyond that the waters are navigable all the way to the Humber estuary.

The weir was as important a feature of the river navigation as the lock and represented just as great a challenge to the engineers. This fine, curving weir and footbridge are on the Thames at Hambledon. Like many navigation weirs the site was chosen because there was already a water mill on the site. The present mill can be seen in the background, but is comparatively modern: there is mention of a mill on the site in the *Domesday Book*. (*Anthony Burton*)

The lock gate had scarcely changed in design or in the way it was manufactured since Leonardo's time. These gates are being built in the Grand Union Canal maintenance depot at Bulbourne in the early twentieth century. (*Waterways Archive Gloucester*)

It was the clothiers of such important textile towns as Leeds, Halifax, Rochdale and Wakefield who clamoured for improvements to the navigation. An Act authorising the work was proposed as early as 1625, but the Bill was rejected; the idea was revived in 1697. An initial survey was carried out by John Hadley, described as 'a great Master of Hydraulicks', accompanied by Ralph Thoresby, a merchant best known for his work as an antiquarian, and the Mayor of Leeds. Thoresby's diary of the expedition noted that 'the ingenious Mr. Hadley questions not its being done, and with less charge than expected, affirming it the noblest river he ever saw not already navigable'. In January 1698, Lord Fairfax introduced a Bill into the Commons to make the Aire navigable from Leeds and the Calder from Wakefield. All the major manufacturing centres supported the Bill, arguing that the navigation was essential for their trade, and quoting the terrible condition of the roads in evidence. The Leeds petition, for example, pointed out that goods had to be taken 22 miles to Rawcliffe, then the nearest point on the navigable section of the Aire, 'the expense whereof is not only very chargeable, but they are forced to stay two months sometimes while the roads are passable to market, and many times they receive considerable damage, through the badness of the roads by overturning.'

The Act was passed in May 1699 and Hadley was appointed Chief Engineer at an annual salary of 400 guineas, roughly £45,000 at today's prices. To overcome a rise of 68ft in 30 miles to Leeds, ten locks were built, and the rise of 28ft in the 12 miles to Wakefield required four locks. The arrangement was typical of river navigations of the time. This involved building a weir across the river and bypassing this with a short artificial cutting containing the lock. No one considered a joined-up system, so individual waterways had locks built to an appropriate size for the barges already in use in that area. In the case of the Aire & Calder Navigation this meant locks 58ft long by 15ft wide that could take the sailing barges of the Humber – the Humber keels.

There were many similar schemes throughout Britain and Ireland, but individual engineers had their own ideas. Some rivers presented far greater problems than those found on the Aire & Calder. One of the most problematic was the Kennet Navigation, from Newbury to the Thames at Reading. The natural river fell 138ft in less than 20 miles. The first engineer employed when work got under way following the passing of the Act of 1715 took the easiest way out. Mill weirs were already in place on the river and he simply put locks next to those and left the river to make its own way to the Thames. This proved totally unsatisfactory and one of the principal owners of the canal, a Newbury maltster, arranged for his son John Hore to take over the works. Hore took a very different approach. There were now eighteen wide locks, all set in artificial cuttings that were so extensive that they represented 11½ miles of the total 18½ miles of the whole navigation. It was now more canal than it was river. The locks had to take the typical large barges in use on the Thames, and Hore used the same technique as on the Exeter Canal, building turf-sided locks. Two of these still survive, with the upper part of the lock being sloping, grassy banks.

Theoretically, the new navigation offered a far wider trade route along both the Kennet and the Thames. The engineering problems had been solved, but the planners had not taken account of the rivalry between the different traders. When William Darvall, a barge owner from Maidenhead, tried to bring his vessels all the way to Newbury, he received bloodthirsty threats in a letter simply signed 'wee Bargemen'. Dated 10 July 1725, it began: 'Mr Darvall wee Bargemen of Redding thought to Acquaint you before 'tis too late, Dam You, if y. work a bote any more to Newbury wee will Kill You if ever you come any more this way. Wee was very near shooting you last time, wee went with to pistols and was not too Minnets too Late.' Perhaps assuming Darvall might think a murder threat was implausible, they continued by saying that if they found the boat at Newbury, they would bore holes in it and sink it. It is hard to believe this now placid waterway was once the scene of such violence. There are no records of whether Darvall heeded the warnings, but neither are there any reports of murders and sinkings.

With the Kennet Navigation, we have a waterway that is more artificial than natural, but it was almost half a century before Britain acquired a canal that was built entirely independently from any natural river or stream. That was certainly not the case in continental Europe. It was here that a new age of canals would be born.

Chapter 3

Canal Cities

Many of the great cities of the world developed either as seaports or on navigable rivers. Some improved on the natural waterways by building canal networks that became so extensive as to serve as defining features of those cities. Most people will put Venice at the top of the list, but it is very much an exception. There is very little evidence of the earliest settlements, but there is general agreement that before the days of the Roman Empire the large expanse of marshy land of the Venetian Lagoon was occupied by fishing communities, living in houses built on stilts. With the attacks on cities of the Roman Empire by forces from northern Europe, many fled to the Lagoon as a place of safety, and the modern city grew. The new citizens looked for rather more substantial houses, and built them on wooden piles to raise them above water level. They created a myriad of small islands, and the inlets and channels became the main means of getting around. As time went on, these natural waterways became too shallow and narrow to take the increasing traffic, so many were dredged and their sides reinforced with stone. One of these natural waterways was a river that carved a great S-shape through Venice, and this became the Grand Canal. In other words, the canals of Venice are not canals in the sense of being entirely man-made, but rather more akin to river navigations. Other cities created entirely artificial systems.

Amsterdam, like so many places in the Netherlands, was developed on reclaimed land on the banks of the Amstel River, where it joined the IJ, an arm of the Zuider Zee. The marshy ground was drained with a system of dykes and dams or levees – the main earthwork surrounding the area was the Amstel Dam, which gave the developing town its name, and Dam Square is still the heart of the modern city. As elsewhere, the dykes were used for transport as well as drainage. The settlement developed as an important port and at the end of the fifteenth century the Singel Canal was built from the waterfront on the IJ Bay to the Amstel River, to enclose the city. It was mainly intended as a defensive moat and at first it was forbidden to build outside the canal. However, by the end of the sixteenth century, Amsterdam was prospering as an international port and major shipbuilding centre. Its importance grew following the establishment of the East India Company in 1602, which brought a lucrative trade in spices to Europe. It was followed in 1621 by the West Indies Company, which also had a prosperous but less innocent trade – slaves from Africa. The city could no longer be contained within the Singel, so the city fathers, rather than allow uncontrolled growth, planned an extensive new city based on concentric canals.

Work began with the building of a new outer defensive canal, the Singelgracht, designed by Daniel Stalpaert. Once completed, it left a large area between that and the older Singel for development. Instead of being left to the sort of higgledy-piggledy patterns of streets and houses that characterised many developing towns in the medieval period, it was carefully planned. The project, designed by Hendrick Jacobszoon Staets, involved draining the land and building three more concentric canals to attach the new city area to the new port that was growing inside the Singel. The land between the canals would be drained and building plots sold along the new waterways. All three canals were dug simultaneously, starting at the southern end. The driving force behind the enterprise was the wealthy merchant class, who supervised the work and drew up building regulations in what was an important early example of urban planning, which was widely followed.

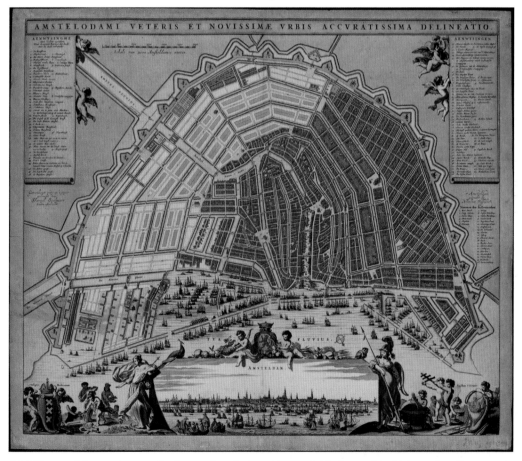

A 1662 map of the canal system for Amsterdam designed by Daniel Stalpeart, in which a series of concentric canals defined new areas for development for the city and set an outside defensive boundary. The map also shows how the canals followed roughly along the lines of old fields and their surrounding dykes. The busy scene depicted at the foot of the map also demonstrates how the enlargement gave Amsterdam the much broader waterfront that was essential for its increased trade. (*Rijk Museum, Amsterdam*)

The innermost canal is the Herengracht, roughly translated as the Lords' Canal. Here the land prices were highest but most sought after. It was considered so prestigious to own property here that the wealthiest citizens bought double plots on which they built some of Amsterdam's grandest houses, many of which still stand. This very fashionable area exuded wealth and became known as the Golden Bend. The Keizersgracht – Emperor's Canal – is next in the series, and the third is the Prinsengracht, the Prince's Canal, which is the widest. The system was completed by radial canals, one of which was the Brouewrsgracht, named much as it sounds after the breweries built on its banks. This was also an area of large warehouses and ships' stores, and was home to many officials of the East India Company. The canals gave Amsterdam its unique atmosphere, in which there was little distinction between commercial and domestic buildings. The Verversgracht, later Zwanenburgwal, was originally named after the dyers and the thriving textile industry along its banks – but it was also to be the home of arguably the country's greatest artist, Rembrandt. UNESCO has designated the Amsterdam Canal District a World Heritage Site, citing that 'Amsterdam was seen as the realisation of the ideal city that was used as a reference urban model for new cities around the world.'

This painting of 1672 by the Dutch artist Gerrit Berckheyde shows the Herengracht, or Lord's Canal, in Amsterdam. This part of the canal became known as The Golden Bend because it attracted the wealthiest citizens to buy land and build along its banks. The opulence and grandeur of the houses is clear from the picture, and many of the buildings still survive: The Golden Bend is still golden. (*Rijk Museum, Amsterdam*)

On the other side of the world, a city was to be developed that had characteristics of both Amsterdam and Venice. In 1782, King Rama I of Thailand decided to establish a new capital along the eastern bank of the Chao Phraya River. He named it Krung Thep Maha Nakhon, which proved too much for Europeans and they renamed it Bangkok, although it remains Krung Thep to the Thai. The original settlement near the river mouth was defined by a canal that acted as a moat, together with a defensive wall. Within the wall, the area was dominated by temples and the homes of the Chinese community; the area outside was a mixture of residential areas and farmland. As in Amsterdam, an imposing new canal, some 20m wide, was added outside the original one, also acting as a defensive moat, leaving an area in between the two for development. The names of the two canals can be translated as the Former City Moat Canal and the City Moat Canal. The two canals were joined by radial canals, known as Lots. There was one other major canal, the Mahanak, which ran out from the City Moat Canal into the countryside. It had an important role in bringing produce into the new city.

Like Amsterdam, Bangkok was planned around a system of canals, which were constructed in the eighteenth century. They are called *klons*, and even in the twentieth century they remained vital to the life of the city. The photograph, taken in 1961, shows two important aspects of life on the *klons*. Houses were built right alongside the waterways, which were the main transport routes, for the city had very few roads, and the *klons* were vital for bringing supplies in from the countryside. Many of the boats in the picture are full of produce for sale in one of the many floating markets. (*SAS Scandinavian Airlines*)

The whole scheme was completed in 1785 and the canals defined the different parts of the city. The area inside the Former City Moat Canal was the centre of government, with the Grand Palace at its heart and important government buildings. Between that canal and the outer ring, the Lots divided the area into three sectors: one for high court officials, another for the lower government ranks and a third for foreigners. Development spread outside the City Moat Canal more haphazardly.

Although the canal system was devised partly as a defensive and town planning system, it was also as a means of controlling water levels, as Bangkok sits on a flood plain. They were to provide the main transport system for the city. Houses crowded along their banks, and a large part of the population lived in floating homes. Produce was brought in and sold in floating markets. They also, like the Venetian Canals, were the thoroughfares of the city. Everything moved by water. There were no roads in Bangkok during the first century after its creation, only raised walkways and all the bridges across the canal complex had to be lifted whenever boats passed. As the waterways were permanently busy, this must have been a huge inconvenience, and made travel by boat all the more attractive. The canals are still in use, but no longer dominate the city; but Bangkok can certainly claim to be one of the great canal cities of the world.

Bangkok has been called, not unreasonably, the Venice of the East: the title Venice of the North is usually given to St. Petersburg. The city was born out of conflict, the war between Sweden and Russia at the beginning of the eighteenth century. The Russian forces under the Tsar Peter the Great took the Swedish fortress of Nyenschantz at the mouth of the Neva. It was in too bad a condition to be repaired so a new fortress was constructed on the island of Zayachy Ostrov ('Hare Island'). Completed in 1703 it was named the Fortress of Peter and Paul and it was the start of what would become the city of St. Petersburg. The Tsar chose the site for his new capital not only for its strategic position, but also because it opened up routes with Western Europe. Peter had travelled widely and was determined to bring Russia into the modern world: in particular he had studied the shipyards of Europe and saw his new capital as the centre around which a Russian industry could develop. But before his grand plans could be realised, he had to drain the marshy land on which he could build.

The work would involve a vast army, mainly made up of serfs. Accommodation was poor and the climate can be fierce, especially in winter when temperatures can drop to -10°C or even lower. The workers suffered from lack of food, terrible housing and long hours. No one kept records of the casualties, but it has been estimated that thousands died in creating the city. They dug canals, cleared land and straightened and embanked rivers. They transformed an entire landscape.

Peter the Great's original plans envisaged a city in which the majority of traffic would move along the rivers and canals, which became the main arteries for building. The first settlements spread out along the Neva, which was straightened and its banks reinforced

The canals of St. Petersburg were mainly built in the early eighteenth century during the reign of Peter the Great. Today they have become as popular with tourists as those of Amsterdam. This boatload of sightseers on the Griboedov Canal is passing the ornate Church of Our Saviour of the Spilled Blood, a name that refers to the assassination of Tsar Alexander II near this spot. (*St. Petersburg Tourist Board*)

with wooden piles. A network of canals and canalised rivers was developed that defined the new city and its limits. The Moyka River was the first to be enclosed between granite banks, a system that soon spread to the other rivers and canals, including the Neva, and became one of the characteristic features of the city's waterways. The outer limit was fixed by the Fontanka River. That was not its original name: Fontanka is a fountain and the name was given in the 1730s, when aqueducts from the river were built to take water to feed the city's fountains. Beyond the river was a tract of wild forest, home to roving bands of brigands, which was why police stations were built all around the periphery to protect travellers.

A canal was built between the Fontanka and Moyka, more or less parallel to them. The Griboedov is narrow and twisting, but famous for the picturesque buildings along its banks. The best known is the Church of Our Saviour of the Spilled Blood, which got its exotic name because it stands close to the spot where Alexander II was assassinated by anarchist bombs. The canals were not just built for commerce; they were intended to be part of the

The St. Petersburg canals have always been noted for their very attractive features, as exemplified by the beautiful wrought ironwork on these railings on the Denidov Bridge. (*Alexei Karprianov*)

beautification of the city. The short Swan Canal, for example, joins two attractive open spaces: the Summer Garden and the Field of Mars.

A distinguishing feature of the St. Petersburg and the other city canal systems already described is that the waterways were seen as essential features that were to be as attractive as they were useful. The nearest thing to a canal city in Britain is Birmingham, which often boasts of having more miles of canal than Venice. But here the situation was very different. The Birmingham canal system was always seen as useful rather than attractive, something to be hidden away behind back streets. Older readers may remember when Gas Street Basin, for example, was a secret enclave, hardly detectable unless you arrived by boat. Access from the road was down steps that curled round a high brick wall that shut off the view. The only clue that there might be anything interesting behind the wall was a red wooden hatch – an indication that firemen could open it up and push their hoses through to suck up water. Rather than seeing the canals as assets, they were largely regarded as handy places to deposit supermarket trollies and dead dogs. They may have played a vital role in developing the city's industries, but they were not seen as attractions.

The old world of the Birmingham canal system was typified by Gas Street Basin, once tucked away unseen behind high brick walls and warehouses. It still retains much of its old atmosphere, enhanced by traditional narrow boats and some of the old surviving buildings beside the lock. The lock itself is very shallow and was constructed to form a barrier between the Worcester & Birmingham Canal and the Birmingham Canal. (*Anthony Burton*)

New developments have transformed the Birmingham canals. The Mailbox development, named after the old Post Office sorting centre that once stood on the site, stands close to Gas Street Basin beside the Worcester & Birmingham Canal. This section of the canal is now lined with popular bars and restaurants. (*Visit Birmingham*)

Change began in the late twentieth century with the development of the area at the top of the Farmer's Bridge flight, where old buildings were restored and a new canalside pub built. But it is only in the last few years that everything has been transformed. Those of us who have been travelling the Birmingham canals for many years scarcely recognise the system today. New buildings of glass and steel stand at the water's edge and the banks in the city centre now bustle with life, lined with bars and cafés. Perhaps now, two and a half centuries after it got its first canal, Birmingham can truly be added to the list of genuine canal cities.

Chapter 4

Coming of Age

It was in seventeenth-century France that canal engineering entered a new age of ambitious projects requiring unprecedented engineering works, beginning with the Canal de Briare. Plans were drawn up as early as 1603 for a canal to link two of the country's most important waterways: the Seine and the Loire. The idea was to improve the little River Trezée from the point where it joined the Loire at the village of Briare, so that it was navigable for 16km. At the opposite end, the River Loing was to be made navigable for some 45km from its junction with the Seine near Montargis. This left a gap in between that was to be closed by a canal crossing the watershed in a 12m deep cutting. The plans were approved and tenders were invited for completing the work that was to involve constructing a total of 48 locks, roughly 27m long and 4.8m wide. The canal was to be 12m wide and 1.4m deep. It seemed feasible, and the contract was awarded to Hugues Cosnier, an engineer born in Tours in 1573.

When Cosnier began his own survey of the proposed route he discovered there had been a major error in the original plans. The plans assumed that the two rivers were at the same height above sea level at the points where they were to be joined: they were not and the difference was a substantial 12m. Not only was this a major surveying error but also no means had been provided for supplying the summit with water. This is essential for any canal that joins two watersheds. A vessel travelling along a canal with a summit such as this climbs up one side by means of locks. To fill the first lock, the water is drawn from the section of canal – the pound – between that lock and the next and so on right up to the top, when the final lockfull has to be drawn from the summit itself. Similarly, when descending the other side, the first lock has to be filled from water in the summit level. In other words, each boat crossing the summit uses two lockfulls of water, which if not replaced leaves the summit dry. As originally planned, the canal was inoperable and a further problem was that no allowance had been made for flooding on the rivers.

Cosnier's new plans were radically different.

The idea of making the rivers navigable was abandoned, and instead Cosnier proposed making a true canal all the way from Briare to Montargis. The Trezée valley would only be followed for 11km, and from that point the canal would head north to a plateau and a 6km summit level. At the same time he proposed building larger locks using substantial masonry. Another engineer, Jean Fontaine, approved them and passed them to the Duke of Sully.

The Canal de Briare in the Loire district of France was a pioneering venture, involving many imposing engineering features. Construction began in 1604 and was completed in 1642, after a long period when work stopped altogether, and the final construction phase only began in 1638. This painting by the nineteenth-century French landscape artist Henri-Joseph Harpignies gives a good impression of the grand scale. (*Anthony Burton*)

Sully had enjoyed a successful career in the military before being appointed by Henry IV to take charge of the country's financial affairs. He was later made Grand Commissioner for Public Works, in charge of roads and waterways. He also approved the plans and arranged for 6,000 soldiers to be seconded to build the new canal. Sully took a personal interest in the progress of the works, making regular visits and even shared his enthusiasm with the King, who made a royal visit accompanied by the Queen.

Work started in 1604 and continued at a good pace. Over the next few years, more than 40km of the 55km canal had been completed and thirty-five substantial locks had been built. These were far more substantial than any allowed for in the original plan, with 2m thick masonry walls and devices that were still a novelty at the time: sluices within the lock chamber, ground sluices, as well as openings in the gates. Where the old plans called for falls of about 1m on average, Cosnier had been far bolder and the largest of the locks had a fall of more than 4m. Yet, because of the new ground sluices, operation still took only ten minutes. His boldest venture was in the sharp drop from the plateau to join the River Loign at Rogny. Here, instead of individual locks, he arranged seven interconnected locks as a staircase: for a boat starting at the top, the bottom gate of the first lock would also be the top gate of the next lock, and so on to the bottom – a total fall of 20m. He had already laid plans for supplying the summit with water, by means of a feeder from a small lake at the head of the River Trezée, the Étang de la Gazonne, that would act as a reservoir. The end was in sight, but a violent change in French politics brought everything to a halt. Henry IV was assassinated and Sully, whose policies may have been sound but whose overbearing manner had made him many enemies, was forced to resign in January 1611.

A commission was set up to decide what to do next, and despite describing the work already done as 'nearly perfect', the project was abandoned. Cosnier offered to finish the work at his own expense in exchange for collecting the tolls during the first six years of operation. His proposal was rejected and the canal languished until 1628 when another survey was carried out by yet another engineer, M. Francini, and the architect Jacques Lemercier. Not much is known about Francini, but Lemercier became famous for his buildings in Paris, notably the reconstruction of the Louvre, including the prominent Pavillon de l'Horloge. They recommended completing the work, but were concerned that the water supply would be inadequate at the summit level. They proposed another feeder from an intake on the Loing to another small lake that would again act as a reservoir.

The most impressive feature of the Canal de Briare was the seven-lock staircase that brought the canal down the steep slope to join the Loire at Rogny. Having all the locks interconnected in this way was new and was the work of the original engineer employed on the canal, Hugues Cosnier. The locks were bypassed, when the Briare canal was connected directly to the Canal Lateral de Loire by an aqueduct over the river. (*Anthony Burton*)

Although Cosnier had been busy on other projects in the meantime, he was still anxious to see this, his most prestigious project, to a conclusion. He volunteered to construct the feeder channel in exchange for the payment of the rest of his fee that the government had owed him all those years. This was agreed, but Cosnier died in 1629 aged just 58. He had been a tireless enthusiast for canal construction and among his unrealised dreams was a ring of canals circling Paris. Although not quite completed during his lifetime, the Canal de Briare remains an impressive monument to his originality and ability. Once again the work was abandoned.

In 1638 work finally got under way again when Guillaume Boutheroue and Jacques Guyon obtained letters patent from Louis XIII to complete the works. The actual construction was entrusted to Boutheroue's brother François. His first task was to restore the damage done by decades of neglect. He built the remaining locks and the feeder channel from the lake by the Loing. The feeder channel was constructed with an accuracy that would have impressed even the Roman hydraulic engineers, with a fall of just 165cm in 21km.

The canal was a great success, with the company formed by Boutheroue and Guyon regularly receiving dividends of 13 per cent. Among the more mundane and important trades in timber and coal, there was also a flourishing business in bringing wine from the great vineyards of Burgundy and Languedoc to the cities of the north. By the middle of the eighteenth century there were about 500 wine barges working on the canal, each of them bow-hauled by men. Briare grew in importance and developed a handsome canal basin, but it was destined to be overtaken by events. In 1860 the canal was taken over by the state and it was decided to join it to the Canal Latéral à la Loire. In the 1890s the latter was extended by a very impressive aqueduct across the Loire, then continued south for 2.6km to join the Briare. As a result, the section down to the old basin was gradually abandoned and Cosnier's masterpiece, the seven-lock staircase, survives only as dry, empty chambers, retained as an industrial monument.

It is worth noting, even if the chronology is upset, that the French have persevered with their use of canals with far more diligence than the British. The Briare and the Latéral now form part of the Bourbonnais system of canals that link the Seine to the Saône, forming part of a north-south system that crosses from coast to coast. The Briare is just one of many canals improved in the latter part of the twentieth century as we shall see shortly.

The usefulness of the Briare Canal was greatly increased by the construction of a short cut between the Loire at Orléans and the Loing at Montagris. The Canal d'Orléans was started in 1682 and completed in 1692. It was 74km long with twenty-eight locks, but for much of its length runs over a flat plateau at the summit. As with the Briare this needed to be supplied with water, which involved building a very long feeder, 32km long, with a fall of little more than a metre through its whole length. The canal fell into disuse, but for many years it was an important part of the timber trade. It is currently being restored for leisure use and is partially open.

The nineteenth-century aqueduct across the Loire at Briare. Built in the 1890s, the water is carried in a 662m long steel trough. The masonry abutments with their elaborate plinths and carvings were the work of one of the most famous engineers of the day, Gustav Eiffel, designer of the famous tower in Paris that bears his name. (*Missot*)

The Canal de Briare's days as a busy commercial waterway have ended, and today it is a peaceful canal enjoyed by holiday boaters. (*Anthony Burton*)

The Briare set a new standard for canal construction and introduced many important innovations. But one seventeenth-century canal stands above all others, not just for the sheer scale of its operation but for its importance in the whole story of canal development – the Canal de Languedoc or, as we know it today, the Canal du Midi.

The idea of a canal that would cut across the whole of France from the Mediterranean to the Atlantic was not new. There was an obvious route to follow that would link the Garonne and the Atlantic port of Bordeaux to the Aude that flowed through Toulouse to the Mediterranean. In the early sixteenth century, Francis I was not only King of France but also ruled over Milan. He was impressed by Milan's canal connections and invited the engineer who had done much of the work, Leonardo da Vinci, to accompany him back to France. Leonardo looked at various routes, appears to have favoured the Garonne-Aude link and proposals were put forward on just how this could be achieved. The first suggestion was for a canal from Toulouse to Carcassonne, put forward by Nicolas Bachelier with a colleague, Arnaud Casanove. Their plans described a lock-free canal together with improvements to the Garonne, either by using the river itself or by building a parallel canal to Bordeaux. Francis I approved the plans, but they were never carried out, and were never really practical.

The plans were dusted off in 1598, when the Duc de Sully ordered a new survey from a Dutch engineer with a very un-Dutch name – Humphrey Bradley. His plans were even less acceptable than Bachelier's and Sully abandoned the idea, turning his attention to the realisable scheme that became the Briare Canal. The great difficulty of finding a route between the two rivers lay in the very dry section at the summit, where there was no obvious way of supplying the canal with water. The solution was eventually found by a man with no previous engineering experience, Pierre-Paul Riquet.

The statue of Pierre-Paul Riquet in Toulouse, erected to honour the man who was the driving force behind the construction of the Canal du Midi that ran from here to Carcassonne. He originally worked as a collector of the salt tax, a lucrative position that allowed him to retire in 1654 aged 50. Instead of idling away his remaining days, he was soon at work surveying the route for the proposed canal. (*Anthony Burton*)

Riquet was born at Béziers in 1604. The family, originally from Florence, were wealthy and influential and Riquet improved his own position aged 18 when he married Catherine de Milhau. She came to him with a dowry big enough to allow him to buy a chateau and estate, aptly named Bonrepos, near Toulouse. In 1630, thanks to family influence, he was appointed as collector of the salt tax for Languedoc. Salt was an essential commodity, not just for seasoning but also for preserving food in the days before refrigeration. Tax rates were high – and hugely unpopular – but the collector received a commission on what he gathered in. Riquet was soon promoted from local collector to collector for the entire province and made a fortune. He went into partnership with his brother-in-law Paul Mas as a military contractor, and made even more money, enough to retire aged 50 and buy a town house in Toulouse to add to his country estate. In modern France he would have been a euro multi-millionaire. He could have lived the quiet life of a country gentleman but instead devoted all his energies to canal construction. His work as tax collector involved travelling all over that region of France, so he knew the country intimately and recognised the great value a canal would bring. He was also sure such a scheme was practical.

There were various alternative routes being canvassed at the time, one of which had a great deal of backing. This involved a canal from the summit to head northwards via the Rivers Agoût and Tarn to the Garonne. Riquet preferred a canal that would begin at Toulouse. But whichever route was chosen, there was still that awkward problem to overcome – how to supply the summit with water.

Riquet had always preferred his country home, Bonrepos, to the town and got on well with the local villagers. It was to one of these men he turned for help. Pierre Campmas was a *fontainier*, literally translated as the man in charge of springs. He was responsible for looking after water supplies in the district so had invaluable knowledge of all the local watercourses. They set out together to explore the summit level, first establishing the point on the watershed where one set of streams flowed east, the others west. This was the Col de Narouze and the nearest sources of water were the streams that fell down the southern slopes of the Montaigne Noire. Riquet realised that these alone would not answer the question and he conceived of damming one or more of the narrow mountain valleys to create reservoirs.

Riquet was astute and visionary, but he was certainly not a qualified engineer and he needed someone who could turn his plans into practical realities. A young man called François Andréossy was recommended by his friend the Bishop of Castres, Monsignor d'Anglure de Bourlemont. Andréossy had studied science and engineering in Paris and had visited Italy in 1660 to see the canal works there. Like Riquet he was convinced that canals would be of ever-greater importance and was anxious to be involved in a major project – and there was no more major scheme than that of the Canal du Midi.

There has been controversy as to who should take the credit for building the canal. There are two separate accounts of the construction, written by descendants of the two men and, not surprisingly, each give the laurels to their own ancestor. L.T.C. Rolt in his excellent history of the canal, *From Sea to Sea,* first published in 1973 and updated by David Edwards-May in 1994, discusses the issue at length. He plumps for Riquet on the grounds that it was his idea and if it had failed he would have had to take the blame so, as it succeeded, he should take the credit. But does there have to be a choice? The idea was certainly all Riquet's, but it could only become a reality with the expertise of his young associate. With such a magnificent venture there is honour enough to share.

Riquet had the support of his old friend Bourlemont who had recently been appointed as Archbishop of Toulouse and now had considerable influence. It was at his suggestion that Riquet wrote to the King's chief minister, Jean-Baptiste Colbert, in November 1662. One of the more surprising aspects of the letter is Riquet's apology for it being clumsily written. He writes that he knows neither of the scholarly languages of the time – Latin and Greek – and admits that his French isn't very good either. In fact he used the local language of Languedoc, Occitan. The main point he wants to get across is that he had a solution to the problem that had scuppered all previous schemes – how to supply the summit with an adequate water supply. He had calculated that the River Sor flowing out of the mountains is 16½m above the summit level and that the river is only 1,500 paces away from a brook known as the Lampy, which in turn connects with other brooks. It would be a simple matter to connect these to provide sufficient water to supply a canal 16½m wide and 1.80m deep. These are generous dimensions, but the canal was not intended just for inland barge traffic: one of its main purposes was to provide a route for coastal shipping to avoid the long and expensive journey round Gibraltar.

Colbert was an ambitious man who was anxious to turn rural France into a modern industrial nation. He was well aware that good communications were the key to success, so the scheme appealed. Riquet and the Archbishop were invited to Paris, arriving in style in the Archbishop's private coach. The meeting was a success and Colbert began getting official approval. He approached Louis XIV who was enthusiastic and authorised a Royal Commission to investigate the proposal. Like most such commissions it was made up of dignitaries, most of whom knew nothing of the subject upon which they were to pronounce judgement. The exception was Henri de Boutheroue, whose father had completed the work on the Briare Canal. Together he and Riquet finalised the plans for the new canal, which was even more ambitious than Riquet had originally planned.

In the new version, the canal would no longer have a terminus at Carcassonne. It would be extended to the Mediterranean at Étang de Thau, where a new port was to be created, originally called Cette but now Sète. Riquet proposed building a whole string of reservoirs, but eventually the system was simplified. There were to be two main feeder canals, or rigoles: the Rigole de la Montaigne, 24km long, rising high in the hills, which would connect with the main feeder, the 35km Rigole de la Plaine, which would meet the summit at the Col de Naurouze. As well as the natural springs

The first problem Riquet had to solve was how to provide water to supply the summit level of the Canal du Midi. He found what he needed in the rivers that flowed off the slopes of the Montaigne Noire. To ensure there was always sufficient water available, he arranged for the building of a vast dam across the Laudot at St. Ferréol. The photograph shows the dam today, rising 42m above the bed of the river. Water from the reservoir held behind the dam was fed to the canal through narrow channels, the rigoles. (*Anthony Burton*)

and streams feeding the rigoles, there was to be a dam across the Laudot at St. Ferreol to create a large reservoir.

The Commissioners niggled away at details for almost a year and, in particular, they doubted the success of a feeder from the Sor being practical. Riquet's bold response was to prove its practicality by digging the feeder at his own expense. Not surprisingly, the Commissioners agreed and sent their approval on 27 May; by July Riquet had worked out a plan. Instead of taking a direct route, which would have involved costly earthworks, he followed the natural contours of the land – a technique that would be used by later generations of canal engineers. This saved a lot of work – and a lot of Riquet's money – and in October of that year the waters of the Sor had reached the summit. It seemed that there were now no more obstacles and work could get under way, but Riquet had not allowed for the cautious workings of the official mind. Another committee was set up to decide who should pay for what. Eventually it was agreed that the state would buy the land, the Province of Languedoc would be authorised to use revenue from the salt tax to pay for construction and, for his contribution, Riquet and his successors would collect the tolls. At last, in October 1666, the King issued an edict authorising construction, which was to be completed in eight years at a cost of 3,360,000 livres, roughly 17 million euros at today's prices.

By winter 1667, there were 12,000 'head' at work. This curious figure was calculated on the basis of both men and women being employed: each man counted as one head, but three women were required to make up two heads. In fact, men represented by far the greater number of workers. The first task was to build the water-supply system. The most important work was the construction of the dam at St. Ferreol. This was to be a massive structure, rising 42m above the bed of the Laudot, with a base that was 140m thick and with a curved crest with a total length of 780m. Everything had to be built by hand, with two outer stone walls, an inner core wall and the spaces between were then packed with earth. Most of the labour of bringing earth for the core onto the site was done by the female workers carrying it in wickerwork baskets. Riquet was immensely proud of this structure and the area around it was landscaped to show it off. The slopes below the dam were planted with trees, the overflow was turned into a series of cascades and the water pressure created an imposing fountain at the bottom of this ornamental parkland. At the base of the dam is a tunnel, known as the arch to the entrance to hell. It is certainly dramatic, but hardly infernal. It provides access to sluices, which wash silt away from the reservoir high above. The various rigoles were not that dramatic, but they too included major engineering works, including a 120m long tunnel. They were built to generous dimensions, and for a time were used by small boats.

Work now began on the canal itself. The workers were organised into twelve divisions, each division having a supervisor. More engineering challenges soon appeared. Five deep locks were to be built at the Toulouse end. To accommodate coastal craft the locks, a

The overflow from the dam was formed into this series of ornamental waterfalls, turning the surroundings into a delightful park with a fountain also fed from the reservoir at the bottom. (*Anthony Burton*)

hundred of them, were built to generous dimensions, mostly 30m long by 5.6m wide. The first locks were begun with conventional rectangular chambers, but one of them collapsed so Riquet used a different design. The new locks had vertical walls, but curved in plan to resist the pressure of the earth. The various rivers met along the way were originally crossed on the level, which must have been an interesting experience for the boatmen, but were mostly later replaced by aqueducts. The Cesse crossing was replaced by a three-arched aqueduct shortly after the opening of the canal. The grandest of the aqueducts, across the River Orb, was built as recently as 1857 and is a magnificent structure of seven arches, with an arcade of smaller arches above carrying the masonry trough.

There were specific technical problems to overcome. In places the canal had to be dug through porous material and made watertight. The solution was puddling. This involved making a semi-fluid mixture of clay and water, which was stamped onto the ground and added in layers until it formed a perfect seal. Other difficulties had nothing to do with the works themselves. Financing the project depended on the salt tax income, a tax that the citizens of Roussilon were not merely reluctant to pay but, according to Riquet, resorted to violence to avoid. In a letter to Colbert he described the locals as famously violent and the area as one in which murder was as common as bread and wine, cheerfully adding that his tax collectors were prepared to kill rather than be killed. The money continued to be collected in spite of sporadic riots.

This aerial view shows a typical lock on the Canal du Midi, crowded with pleasure boats. Lock construction was still in its infancy, and Riquet had problems creating conventional locks as the sides tended to collapse under the pressure. To give them extra strength he built the locks with curved sides which, being in effect arches turned on their side, offered greater resistance. (*Edition Laubatièras*)

Work proceeded more slowly than anticipated – a familiar problem with major engineering projects, but one not always understood by officials in Parisian offices. An exasperated Colbert threatened to send in new men to take over. Riquet had just begun to face a unique challenge, driving a tunnel through a hill at aptly named Malpas (bad step). He received word that a Commission was about to descend on the works and if they were dissatisfied then everything would stop until a new organisation was in place. Riquet called in all the men engaged in other work in the district and set them to work tunnelling. As one crew advanced hacking their way through the rock, another crew followed on behind them erecting wooden beams to support the roof. Masons were kept busy lining the side walls. The tunnel is not very long, just 165m, but is of imposing size, more than 7m wide and with the crown of the roof arch 5.8m above the water line. Amazingly, according to legend, all this work was completed in just six days. The tunnel has a distinctly odd appearance even today. The western end is lined and faced by an imposing portal; the eastern end remains as natural rock with an entrance that looks more like the opening to a cave than a canal tunnel. Was this the state of the tunnel when the Commission made the inspection and, once that was over, did Riquet simply leave things as they are, having made his point? There is no evidence one way or another.

The critics were temporarily silenced. However, the approach to the River Orb was so steep they decided that the canal would never reach it. Riquet had already used double locks in other parts of the canal, but this time he produced a truly spectacular solution to the problem – a seven-lock staircase with a total drop of 21.5m in 280m. The critics were confounded. But it was Riquet's final triumph. In October 1680 he died aged 76, just seven months before the canal officially opened. His obituarist compared him to Moses who didn't live to enter the Promised Land.

The opening of the canal on 15 May 1681 was a grand affair, presided over by the Governor of Languedoc. A fleet of cargo boats from the Garonne set off from Toulouse with goods from the fair at Beaucaire, reaching Sète ten days later. It marked the end of one stage of the canal's history. Improvements continued in the following years and included the construction of the Canal Latéral à la Garonne, providing far better communication from the Midi at Toulouse to Bordeaux.

Financially the canal was a great success. At its most active there were some 250 boats using the canal, each capable of carrying loads of about 60 tonnes. There was a regular mail service on the canal, and the mail boats also carried passengers from 1684, with 30,000 a year using the service. By the middle of the nineteenth-century goods traffic had peaked at 110 million tonne-kilometres per annum. But a competition had appeared – the steam railway. To fight it off a new fast mail service was introduced, with teams of horses changed at regular intervals and travelling day and night. The journey time was reduced to 35 hours from Toulouse to Sète. It was all in vain, and in the twentieth century the motor age brought even more fierce competition. By this time the canal was under state control

The aqueduct carrying the Canal du Midi across the River Orb at Béziers. Originally the canal entered the river directly, and boats had to make their way downstream for several hundred yards before joining the next section of canal. This proved dangerous, especially when the river was in flood, and improvements were considered as early as the eighteenth century, including building a tunnel under the river. The solution finally arrived with the construction of the aqueduct, completed in 1858, together with two extra locks to reunite the new and old routes. (*Anthony Burton*)

and there were serious attempts to modernise it to keep trade flowing. Improvements failed to halt the drift of cargo traffic away from the canal, which today thrives as a busy holiday route for pleasure boating. Traffic may have changed, but the canal remains in use more than three centuries after it was built. Riquet would surely have approved. He had originally planned to have an ornate statue of the King placed at the summit where the rigole meets the canal. It was never built, but there is a monument there, not to royalty but to the man who made the canal a reality – Pierre-Paul Riquet.

Canal construction in the seventeenth century was not limited to France. The Prussian ruler Friedrich Wilhelm ordered the construction of a 15-mile waterway to connect the Rivers Sprey and Oder. Completed in 1669, it was the first major canal built in what is now Germany.

A far more complex network was developed in the Netherlands. The whole system of government changed in the 1590s with the formation of the United Provinces, which were largely autonomous. This presented something of a problem when it came to constructing waterways that would inevitably need to cross provincial boundaries – basically little could be done until everyone agreed. The Dutch had been improving their navigation

The Canal du Midi had one very original feature – a tunnel. This early photograph shows the Malpas tunnel in the early part of the twentieth century, and clearly shows how it was carved out of solid rock. No attempt has been made to line most of the tunnel, but today the surroundings have been greatly tidied and no longer have the rough and ready appearance of a century ago. (*Anthony Burton*)

system based on the dykes and rivers for many years, but in the seventeenth century they embarked on the construction of a complex of canals known as *trekvaarten* built specifically for passenger traffic. The first *trekvaart*, joining Haarlem and Amsterdam, was completed in 1631 and was soon followed by other intercity links: Leiden was joined to Haarlem and Delft; Amsterdam to Weesp and Naarden. The new system could take market boats and passenger boats, but not large cargo barges, and they spread throughout the country. Passenger boats (*trekshuits*) ran to a strict timetable. They were generally long and narrow craft, with room for up to thirty passengers. They were pulled by horses, usually ridden by a young boy, and the boats were run by a captain and mate. Going under bridges was a juggling act. The towlines were generally attached to tall masts. The British engineer John Smeaton travelled on one of these vessels and described how they coped. The rope was unhooked, allowed to run over the bridge and caught on the other side, when it could be reattached. The routes were immensely popular. Charles Hadfield in his *World Canals* (1986) gives the number of passengers using the Amsterdam–Haarlem route in the 1660s as 288,000 a year.

Visitors were most impressed. Richard Castle, in an essay of 1730, described the Dutch as having 'exceeded all nations we know of, in works of this kind' and noted that: 'The Province of Holland in effect is but one continued cluster of cities by means of their canals alone.'

One other country built a summit-level canal in the early eighteenth century, a country that is often ignored when discussing the development of canals in the British Isles – Ireland. The impetus for constructing the Newry Canal came with the discovery of an important coalfield in Tyrone, although the idea of a canal had been around for a long time. It looked as if things might really get under way when the Commissioners for Inland Navigation for Ireland were appointed in 1729 and gave their approval. Construction was to be controlled by the Surveyor General, Thomas Burgh, but as he had a financial interest in another coalfield nothing was done. He died, however, the following year, but his successor had more interesting architectural projects to work on, including new parliament buildings, so he in turn handed on the task to Richard Cassels, who fared no better. It seemed that the canal was doomed to fail simply because no one would give it their full attention. Then in 1736 the job was passed to Thomas Steers, a man of considerable experience. Born in 1672, he built Liverpool's first dock and worked on many important navigation schemes, including the Mersey & Irwell and the Weaver. Under his direction, work finally got under way. The 14 mile long canal linked the coalfield, via Lough Neagh and the River Bann to the Irish Sea, allowing coal to be

The British Isles got a canal in the early eighteenth century with the building of the Newry Canal. After a couple of false starts, Thomas Steers was appointed chief engineer in 1736. The canal was designed for barges to bring coal from pits in Tyrone to Lough Neagh and the Irish Sea and had a total of fourteen locks in 14 miles. This early photograph shows the basin and the lock that linked the canal to the open water, with a schooner and a small steamer tied up at the quay. The main trade was in coal for Dublin. (*Michael Pollard*)

taken round the coast to Dublin. There were fourteen locks designed for vessels 44ft long and 15ft 6in beam.

The canal was a success in regard to trade but was not well constructed. The original brick walls of the locks had to be replaced by stone and there were constant problems of water supply at the summit. Thomas Omer was the next engineer brought in to improve matters, and his main contribution was an improvement of the 2-mile section between Newry and the sea lough that allowed large ships to reach the town. Newry profited from its new role as a major port. Nothing on this scale was attempted in mainland Britain for many years.

By the early eighteenth century, canals had spread through many of the countries of Western Europe and were much admired. But among all the schemes, none attracted as much attention as the Canal du Midi. It became a regular stopping off point for young British aristocrats embarking on the Grand Tour, a welcome change for many from an unending diet of antique ruins. Among those impressed was a young Englishman, Francis Egerton, third Duke of Bridgewater. It changed his life and that of his country.

Chapter 5

The Industrial Revolution

Traditionally the starting date for the industrial revolution that was to transform British society is 1760. One reason that date was selected is closely tied to an important development in the world of canals. The story begins with young Francis Egerton, who had an unhappy childhood. His father, the Duke of Bridgewater, died in 1745 when the boy was just 9 years old and his mother soon remarried. He was seen by the family as insignificant and rather stupid. As a younger brother with few prospects, no one bothered much about him and his education was neglected. Then, in 1748, his brother died and Francis was now heir to the dukedom. The family were not happy and even tried to get him declared unfit to take the title but the courts decided otherwise. It became a matter of urgency to fill in the gaps in his education to prepare him for his new role as the third Duke of Bridgewater, hence the suddenly arranged trip to Europe on which he visited the Canal du Midi. The object was to preen him into courtly manners by taking him to Paris, where he was expected to learn the finer points of life in polite society. As a teenager having his first trip abroad he showed more interest in pursuing actresses, a polite name for young ladies who seldom performed on any public stage. He was rapidly whisked off to Italy and the circuit of antique sites and encouraged by his tutor to buy large quantities of statues and artefacts that were then packed up and sent back to England. It is said the crates were never opened.

Back in England as a young man he wooed one of the great beauties of the day, Maria Gunning, young widow of the Earl of Coventry. All was going well, but rumours spread that Maria's sister, the Duchess of Hamilton, was not behaving as she should. The young Duke announced to Maria that she must make a choice: cut her sister out of her life forever or end her relationship with him. Faced with this ludicrous and pompous request, she sensibly chose the latter course. The love affair was at an end and the Duke abandoned the London court forever and vowed never again to have anything to do with women. It was said that he even refused to have female servants. He now devoted himself to improving his estates near Manchester.

Changes were already apparent by the middle of the eighteenth century in Britain. There was a steady movement from country to town and a new demand for basic commodities. The town dwellers could no longer gather firewood from the commons and woodland to heat their homes and now bought coal. And a major new industrial use had been found for the fuel. Early in the century Abraham Darby, the iron master of Coalbrookdale in

There is a well-known and much reproduced illustration of the young Duke of Bridgewater, looking every inch the Georgian dandy, pointing with pride at the Barton aqueduct. In later years, he dressed so plainly that he was often mistaken for one of his own workmen. This sign was photographed outside a pub close to the junction of the Trent & Mersey and Caldon Canals and shows him as he appeared in his later years, but still with the Barton aqueduct in the background. (*Anthony Burton*)

Shropshire, had succeeded in using coal for smelting the ore, by turning it into coke before using it to fire the furnaces. This was good news for the young Duke whose estate included mines at Worsley, only a few miles from the rapidly growing town of Manchester. He could make a handsome profit provided he could get it from pit to customer easily and cheaply. And, of course, he knew the answer already from his trip through France. What he needed was a canal.

The Duke was still in his early twenties and relied heavily on two employees: the brothers Thomas and John Gilbert. Together they laid their plans. To build any canal or upgrade a waterway it was first necessary to obtain an Act of Parliament. This they succeeded in doing, but their proposal was heavily amended. It got them as far as the navigable River Irwell and there it stopped. The Duke applied to the Irwell Navigation for permission to connect his canal to their waterway, but was refused point blank. The old company had a profitable monopoly and saw any addition to the system as a threat. He needed a new plan and he needed help from someone with experience of this sort of work. He was recommended to approach a Derbyshire millwright, James Brindley, who had experience in handling water management problems having recently designed a complex drainage system for the all too appropriately named Wet Earth Colliery.

It is tempting to think of the Duke and Brindley as the British equivalent of Riquet and Andréossy, but the contrasts are more obvious than the similarities. The Duke was a young man, just 23 when he began planning his canal, with no practical experience of running any enterprise. Riquet had reached the end of a highly successful career in businesses of various kinds. This did not necessarily mean that either was prepared for the problems that would arise during canal construction: both men were practically bankrupted at one time. The young Duke was once reported to have been found hiding in a barn from a creditor. Andréossy had studied both science and engineering at university and had travelled widely to gain first-hand knowledge of the latest thinking about the technology of canal construction. Brindley had only a rudimentary education. He remained semi-literate throughout his life. His notebooks show him spelling words phonetically, and with hints at his own Derbyshire accent, so 'luck' became 'louk' and an engine was an 'engon'. His experience was all practical, and not necessarily the worse for that. He was used to working things out for himself, and it was said that when faced with a difficult problem he would retire to a darkened room and lie down until he had it solved in his head. There was no question of making calculations on paper. He was undoubtedly a success in his new career as canal engineer, but there is also a very good case for saying that much of the credit for the successful construction of the Bridgewater Canal lay with the two Gilbert brothers.

In 1760 a new Bridgewater Canal Act was passed, in spite of fierce opposition from the older Irwell Navigation Company. Instead of joining the Irwell, this canal would stride across it on an aqueduct. It is a mark of British insularity that one eminent engineer, when shown the plans, remarked that he had often heard of castles in the air, but this was the first time he had heard of anyone actually trying to build one. The critics were confounded. The canal was built and included what was considered a wholly new invention of Brindley's – the use of puddled clay to keep the bed watertight. As we have seen, this had actually been used in the previous century on the Canal du Midi. The canal was lock free and there was no water supply problem as it was used to help drain the mines at Worsley. There were, however, a few last minute worries. When the water was let into the substantial stone aqueduct, there were worrying signs of cracks. The problem was located. Brindley had been over-cautious and had put in so much puddle that the structure was overstressed. The water was drained out, much of the heavy puddle removed and the problem was solved.

Although river navigations had been improved for many decades and the Sankey Brook Navigation, completed in 1755, was an independent canal in all but name, the Bridgewater created a sensation. The sight of boats on the canal passing over boats on the river was considered so strange that it became a regular stopping off point for sightseeing tours. One tourist, Samuel Curwen, was overwhelmed and declared that he hardly dared walk over the towpath. We can no longer walk over the original aqueduct. It was demolished at the end of the nineteenth century, when the Irwell was incorporated into the Manchester Ship Canal. The original aqueduct did, however, survive long enough to be photographed and we can see that it was a less graceful structure than it appears in contemporary prints and modest compared with later structures.

The Barton aqueduct that carried the Bridgewater Canal across the Irwell Navigation, photographed in 1891, shortly before it was demolished to make way for the Manchester Ship Canal. It is difficult now to see this plain structure as awe inspiring, but when it opened in 1761 it was the wonder of the age and tourists rushed to see the boats on a canal crossing over boats on a river. (*Waterways Archive Gloucester*)

Meanwhile, an extension of the Bridgewater Canal was to be built that would take it south, down to the Mersey at Runcorn. Brindley was again the man in charge and in planning the route he chose a method that was to be a trademark of his canals. Just as Riquet had done when building the rigoles for his canal, Brindley took the line of least resistance, preferring to go around obstacles, rather than through or over them, by following the natural contours. However, when it came to joining the Mersey he had no option: he had to build a flight of locks to join the two waterways. As the basic idea was to make the canal accessible to the traditional trading vessels already in use on the river, the Mersey flats, it was necessary to make each lock large enough to accommodate a single boat. They were made 72ft by 15ft, soundly built of massive stones that, according to one visitor, weighed up to 12 tonnes each.

What visitors to the canal did not realise was that they were only seeing a portion of the whole. Behind the narrow mine entrance at Worsley Delph lay a network of underground canals. Carts brought coal from the face to be loaded into long thin vessels, just 4ft 6in wide. Because of their shape and the prominent ribs they were known as 'starvationers'. Once out of the mine, the vessels were linked together and towed away on the main canal.

The Bridgewater Canal began underground in the Duke's mines at Worsley, just outside Manchester. This crude illustration shows the entrance to the mines and the immense crane used to load stone into a boat. The simple vessels originally used on the canals were long and narrow, known as starvationers, and they could be floated right into the workings to be loaded near the coal face. (*British Museum*)

There was an ingenious method used for unloading the vessels at the Castlefield wharf at the Manchester end of the canal. To raise the cargo to street level, boats were floated under the bottom of a shaft and a water-powered crane lifted the coal to the top.

Whereas the general public came to stare at the engineering marvel, others were much more impressed by a simple statistic – the price paid for Worsley coal in Manchester was halved. Britain was just starting on a great period of transformation. It started in the cotton textile industry, where the preparatory processes of carding and spinning were being taken out of the workers' homes. New machines were installed in mills, powered by water wheels that, by the end of the century, would be replaced by steam engines. The changes created an even greater demand for coal, a fact that famously resulted in the Duke of Bridgewater remarking that a successful canal must have 'coal at the heel of it'. Other traditional industries were also undergoing profound changes and creating their own demands for the new transport system.

Until the middle of the eighteenth century, the Staffordshire potteries, based in and around Stoke-on-Trent, mostly made earthenware using the local dark clay. The only way to produce a white plate, for example, was to cover it with a heavy, opaque glaze. Each item would be made by an individual potter, a skilled craftsman who was in charge of everything from throwing a pot on a wheel to fixing on the handle and finishing with a suitable pattern and glaze. One man who changed all that was Josiah Wedgwood. He wanted to

James Brindley, the former millwright from Derbyshire, was employed by the Duke of Bridgewater as engineer for the Duke's canals. The success of this pioneering venture made him the first choice for new canal companies begun in the 1760s. Here he looks relaxed, with his arm resting on his surveying instrument, but in reality he was leading a highly stressed and active life, moving from project to project. He died in 1772 with several important projects still unfinished. (*City Museum, Stoke-on-Trent*)

appeal to the aristocracy and the new, rapidly developing middle class market. There was a growing enthusiasm for imported porcelain from the Far East and Wedgwood set out to emulate it in earthenware. That would never have been possible with the local clays, so he brought in a much paler clay, available in Devon and Cornwall. To whiten it he mixed the clay with flint that had been heated to a high temperature to make it friable after which it was ground to a fine powder. So he had two new sources of raw material: clay from the West Country and flint from East Anglia. Bringing them overland to Staffordshire would have been ruinously expensive. He was also making delicate ware unsuitable for transportation along the bumpy roads of the time. This was only a part of his innovation: he no longer relied on craftsmen making a single pot then starting work on another. He set up what was, in effect, a primitive version of a production line: one potter throwing, another worker adding handles, someone else doing the decoration and so on. To organise this new workforce he wanted to build a factory designed specifically to streamline the new processes. Obviously the new works would need an efficient transport system to bring in raw materials and take out finished ware. He needed a canal.

Wedgwood became the main promoter for a canal that would cross the country, connecting two great navigable rivers. It would be the Trent & Mersey Canal, with a direct connection with the Trent and joining the Mersey via the Bridgewater Canal. His flints could be shipped round the coast to the Humber and then into the Trent; his clay from

The most important canal on which Brindley was involved after completing the Bridgewater was the Trent & Mersey. The chief promoter was the famous potter, Josiah Wedgwood, who built a new factory alongside the canal at a spot that he named Etruria, after antique pottery that he admired and that he believed, incorrectly, was made by the Etruscans. The site is now part of Stoke-on-Trent. The sketch shows the factory and a working boat out on the water. The factory was later moved and most of the original site was cleared, leaving only the circular domed building in the foreground of this picture. (*Wedgwood P.R. dept.*)

As well as the factory, Wedgwood built a new house for himself and his family, looking out over the canal and the works, Etruria Hall. The enamelled plaque shows the house and canal and the extensive parkland in between. Wedgwood tried to persuade Brindley to provide a sweeping curve at that point, but the engineer would have none of it. Wedgwood declared him an 'inflexible vandal', but the argument did not spoil their genuine friendship. (*Wedgwood P.R. dept.*)

the West Country could be brought to the Mersey. He turned inevitably to the man of the moment, James Brindley. This was a canal on a scale never attempted in Britain before, but it was not the only canal for which he had been signed up as chief engineer. He was also in charge of the Staffs & Worcester that was to link the Trent & Mersey to the River Severn. But it was the Trent & Mersey that gave him his biggest headache.

Ideally the new canals would, like the Bridgewater, be available for the barges already in use on the rivers they connected. The Trent & Mersey, however, had to cross a line of low hills. It was not possible to go around, and there would have been far too many problems, not least water supply, to go over the ridge. The only solution was to go through in a tunnel. But, unlike that at Malpas on the Canal du Midi, this would not be a few hundred yards long: it would have to be about a mile and a half. Brindley baulked at digging a tunnel that would need to be 15ft wide to take the river barges. One has to bear in mind that geology had not yet developed as a science. He had no idea what the ground inside the hill would be like – and he was, in fact, to have some unpleasant surprises. So he simply halved the width, effectively quartering the amount of material to excavate. If you think of

The greatest challenge faced by Brindley was Harecastle Hill that lay right across the route of the Trent & Mersey. The only solution was to build a tunnel. The first canal tunnel at Malpas had been modest, but this would have to be more than a mile long. The first Brindley locks on the Bridgewater had taken vessels of 14ft beam, but building a tunnel to such dimensions was too much. It was designed instead to take vessels just half that width and with a one-way traffic. The photograph shows the low, narrow opening to the now disused Brindley tunnel on the left and the new, improved tunnel built by Thomas Telford to the right. Originally both were used to allow two-way traffic; today only the Telford tunnel is open and traffic is again one-way at a time. (*Anthony Burton*)

the tunnel as being basically circular in cross section, the area is determined by the square of the radius, not as a straightforward multiple of it. The resulting tunnel was low and narrow, with just enough space for one boat and no room left for a towpath. Traffic had to be regulated, with certain hours allocated for travel in each direction. The boats had to be moved by 'legging', the boatman lying on his back and walking his feet against the roof.

Having taken this momentous decision, he now had to decide how the canal would be operated. As the wide barges could not use the tunnel, there were two possible solutions: set up a system in which barges would arrive at either end and then tranship their load to smaller vessels, or not have barges on the canal at all. The latter meant Brindley could save himself a lot of expensive construction. He could halve the width of the locks. His new locks would be half the width of those he had built at Runcorn and a new type of boat was developed for the canal, the narrow boat, roughly 7ft beam and 70ft in length.

As work got under way, Brindley was in demand for still more canals: the Birmingham Canal (from Wolverhampton to Birmingham) and the Coventry Canal were both approved in 1768 and the following year the Oxford Canal Act was passed. Together they would

Once it was decided to build Harecastle tunnel so that it could only be used by vessels roughly 7ft wide, it seemed pointless to build other structures, such as locks, to take wider vessels. As a result, all these early canals were built with narrow locks and a new type of canal boat was born – the narrow boat. This heavily laden narrow boat is being towed on another canal for which Brindley was the chief engineer, the Coventry. (*Miss E. M. Waine*)

form a cross linking the four great rivers of England: Thames, Severn, Trent and Mersey. As this was to be an interconnected system, Brindley decreed that all should be narrow canals, and a pattern was set for canal development in much of Britain. No one was unduly concerned: it still meant that canals were much more efficient than any other transport system known at that time.

Brindley also set his mark on the canals in other ways. He followed his favoured method of contour cutting. For much of the way the routes of these canals wandered apparently aimlessly. Anyone travelling north of Banbury on the Oxford Canal, for example, will at one point find themselves at Wormleighton with a view of an attractive house on a hill in front of them; many minutes later, they will have almost circled the hill and finish up staring

The Brindley canals were all built on the same basic principle. To avoid expensive earthworks, such as cuttings and embankments, they followed the natural contours of the land. In undulating country this could mean a wayward route of extravagant curves, as seen in this aerial view of the Oxford Canal at Wormleighton, north of Banbury. The marks in the field in the foreground are the remains of the moated manor and medieval village. (*Cambridge University Collection of Air Photographs*)

at the back door of the same house. The northern section of the canal was subsequently straightened, but in its original form it was said that boatmen could travel all day and still hear Brinklow clock striking. An even more dramatic example of Brindley's methods is on the Birmingham Canal. This too was straightened, and if you travel it today then you will see several side branches that loop round and rejoin the main canal much further on. These were not built as loops: they are the curving lines of the original waterway.

Brindley led an exhausting life, travelling round all the canals he was being paid to supervise, and often infuriating the companies that felt they were not getting enough of his time. Nothing gave him more trouble than the great tunnel through Harecastle Hill. The act for construction was approved in 1766 and, the following year, the engineer blithely announced that the whole works would be finished in five years. In the event he did not live to see its completion: he died in 1772 and the tunnel finally opened to traffic in 1777; the five years had become eleven. The delays are not too surprising, for nothing on this scale had been attempted on any canal anywhere in the world.

The first stage was to survey the route, setting out the line and using a theodolite to measure the height above the level of the canal bed at various points over the hill. It was then possible to sink a series of shafts from the surface to canal level. Compass directions taken at the surface were transferred to the underground workings, so that men could work from the bottom of the shafts as well as from the two ends. Theoretically, they would then all join together in a straight line. The original tunnel has long since been closed but there are other tunnels on the line and the one at Preston Brook, which is three quarters of a mile long, is still in use. Travelling through it by boat reveals that is very definitely not straight. Thomas Telford was called on in 1822 to inspect the Harecastle tunnel and his report was scathing:

> 'In many places the roof is not more than 6 feet above the ordinary level of the water … in some places it is too narrow, in others crooked, and generally speaking the brickwork which forms the bottom, side & top of the Tunnel is not more than 9 inches thick, it has throughout been made with bad mortar, so that in all the brickwork under water … the mortar is as soft as clay.'

No doubt the criticism is justified, but Brindley and his team were pioneers, struggling under difficult conditions. In some places they met hard rock, which had to be drilled by hand and then blasted with gunpowder; in other spots they met soft ground little better than quicksand. In places the canal ran through coal measures that gave off 'fire damp', the potentially lethal methane gas. Ventilation was supplied by means of a stove and a pipe that sucked out the gas and released it at the surface. Water flooding into the workings was a constant problem. At first, pumps driven by water wheels and a wind pump were used for drainage. When they proved insufficient, Brindley installed a Newcomen engine to do the job. This was an early form of steam engine, but one that used atmospheric pressure rather than actual steam pressure to do its work. The pump rods descending into the workings were suspended from one end of an overhead beam, balanced at its centre. The weight of the rods dragged that end of the beam down. At the other end was a piston suspended from a chain that fitted snugly inside an open-topped cylinder. Steam from a boiler was let into the cylinder and then condensed by spraying it with cold water. This condensed the steam, creating a partial vacuum below the piston. Air pressure now pushed the piston down and, lowering that end of the beam, lifted the pump rods at the other end at the same time. Pressure equalised, the rods dropped again. So the beam bobbed up and down, the pump rods rose and fell and the water was removed. Engines such as this were huge, cumbersome devices and, in terms of the energy that had to be put into the system in the form of heat to raise steam, incredibly inefficient. But they represented the latest in technology at that time, although they were soon made obsolete by the true steam engines designed by James Watt.

This first generation of British canals introduced no specifically new technological advances, although the tunnelling was on a scale never previously attempted. It did, however, differ in several important aspects. The way in which the canals were funded was unlike that used in continental Europe. Apart from the Bridgewater Canal, for which the Duke of Bridgewater himself put up the money, the rest raised the finance by setting up private companies and selling shares. The promoters of these early companies were often men who were more interested in the advantages to their own businesses than in possible dividends, not that they were averse to the latter. Wedgwood acted as treasurer for the Trent & Mersey, a post of considerable importance, but not profitable as he wryly noted when setting out details of the main official appointments:

'James Brindley, Surveyor general   £200 per ann.
Hugh Henshall, Clerk of the Works   £150 per ann. for self & clerk
T. Sparrow Clerk, to the Proprietors   £100 per ann.
Jos. Wedgwood, treasurer at £000 per ann. out of which he bears his own expenses.'

One striking effect of the development was new inland ports where the canals met the major rivers, and goods had to be stored for transhipments between the narrow boats and the river barges. The best known of these new towns is Stourport. An old story repeated in many early canal histories states that the citizens of Bewdley, a thriving port on the Severn, were approached by Brindley who wanted to make the town the terminus of the Staffs & Worcester Canal. They rudely told him to take his 'stinking ditch' elsewhere. So he did. It's a good tale but unfortunately untrue. Documents show that all the petitioning was the other way round: Bewdley wanted the canal, seeing it as increasing their trade. Brindley, however, was much more concerned in finding the easiest route to dig the canal, and that meant following the line of the little River Stour to a point on the Severn downstream from Bewdley. And it was here that Stourport developed. A wide basin was constructed, with river access through both wide barge locks and narrow canal locks. Warehouses were built, with houses for the staff, and traders could be entertained at a new hotel, *The Tontine*. The name derives from the curious custom in which a group of investors put their money into the tontine and the last surviving member of the group got the lot, and the descendants of the other investors got nothing. The other notable new town that grew up at the time was Shardlow, at the Trent end of the Trent & Mersey. One of the most striking features is the former Trent Corn Mill. This was built over a wide arch that spans a spur of the canal so that boats could be loaded and unloaded under cover. Similar buildings were constructed throughout the canal building period in Britain.

New towns were not the only developments. The new industrialists now favoured canalside sites. Wedgwood, the chief promoter of the Trent & Mersey, built a new factory

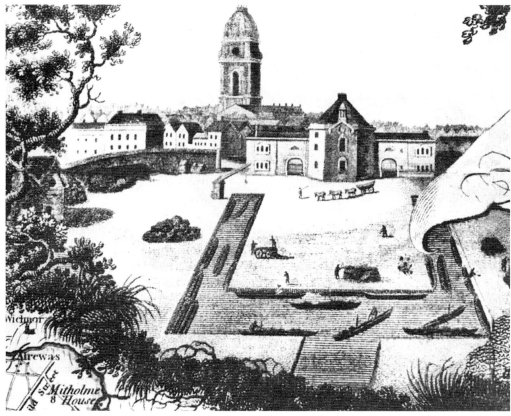

One of the most important, and financially successful, canals was the Birmingham. It attracted industrialists to set up in business along its banks. The most famous was Boulton & Watt who established their new Soho factory for making steam engines alongside the canal, with a short branch leading to an extensive basin. This part of the system is now rarely used, as the new main line was built by Telford on a more direct line, leaving this part as the Soho Loop. (*Jennifer Tann*)

at Etruria together with workers' houses. The only trace of the original works is a small circular domed building near the canal bridge. His own new house, Etruria Hall, looks down on the canal and the works. He tried to persuade Brindley to make an elegant curve in the canal at that point to create a picturesque effect, but the engineer was having none of it. Wedgwood jokingly called him a vandal, but the engineer insisted reasonably on the direct line. Later, when Boulton & Watt began a new factory designed for building steam engines, they did not build it next to Matthew Boulton's existing works on the outskirts of Birmingham, but right alongside the original Brindley canal. It was called the Soho factory and when the new straight line Birmingham Canal was built, this section was bypassed and became known as the Soho Loop.

Brindley was not the only canal engineer at work during the 1760s and 1770s, nor were all built to his ideas as contour canals with narrow locks. The Forth & Clyde Canal did just what its name suggests: it joined those two great Scottish rivers. The engineer was John Smeaton, the man who enthused about Dutch canals, a fact that in itself shows he was more travelled and experienced than Brindley. In fact their backgrounds could hardly have been less similar. Smeaton's father was a lawyer in Yorkshire and, after a grammar school education, he joined his father in the business. He was much happier in his workshop at home than in the office, and taught himself the skills to become a maker of scientific

Other famous engineers working on canals during this period included John Smeaton. He is often described as the father of civil engineering in Britain, responsible for many prestigious structures, including the Eddystone lighthouse, completed in 1759. He was the chief engineer on a canal which, like the Leeds & Liverpool, ran from coast to coast, but this time across Scotland – the Forth & Clyde. (*National Portrait Gallery, London*)

instruments. His interest in science, however, went further than that: he undertook the first scientific examination of wind and water power, studies that won him a Fellowship of the Royal Society. In 1755 he paid the visit to Holland mentioned earlier and soon after that began the move from instrument making to engineering. His best-known early work was the building of the Eddystone lighthouse, which has subsequently been replaced, but the original Smeaton tower has been re-erected on Plymouth Hoe. By the 1760s he had considerable experience of river navigation and drainage schemes when he was invited to visit Scotland to consider building a canal. Inevitably Brindley was also consulted and the pair were at work in 1768. Brindley was already heavily engaged in a large number of projects in England and seems to have rushed to a conclusion that earned a scathing report from Smeaton:

'Mr Brindley recommends to begin at the point of partition, [the summit] because, he says, it is his "constant" practice to do so, and, in the present undertaking, it seems particularly advisable "on many accounts"; but pray, Mr Brindley, is there no way to do a thing right but the way you do? I wish you had been a little more explicit on many accounts: I think you only mention one, and that is to give more time to examine the ends; but pray, Mr Brindley, if you were in a hurry, and the weather happened to be bad, are the works to be immediately stopped when you blow the whistle, till you can come again, and make a more mature examination?'

The work was entrusted to Smeaton and it was a major undertaking, with a summit 150ft above sea level. There was no opportunity for contour canal construction here, and Smeaton showed his mastery by planning a route with a 16 mile long summit, reached by twenty locks from the Forth and nineteen from the Clyde. Like the Canal du Midi, the Forth & Clyde linked two seas and was intended for use by coastal craft up to 68ft 6in long and 19ft 8in beam. The most imposing structure was the Kelvin aqueduct that dwarfed the Barton aqueduct over the Irwell. It is 445ft long and is carried 62ft above the river on four arches. Visitors in the early days witnessed the amazing sight of tall masted ships sailing across it or being bow hauled by a large team of men. The canal work was actually held up for many years because of a lack of funds, so the aqueduct itself was actually the work of Smeaton's successor, Robert Whitworth, and opened in 1790. The 'new town' of Port Dundas was established on the canal approximately 1 mile north of the centre of Glasgow. It was the showpiece of the canal and the company built suitably imposing offices there. One of the first canalside industries to arrive was an equally imposing whisky distillery.

One other important canal that was built to a different standard from that of the Midland network was the Leeds & Liverpool, authorised in 1770. Work began at the Leeds end under the direction of John Longbotham. Brindley once again was involved in the early days, but was far too busy to take over the demanding role of chief engineer for such a vast enterprise.

The most majestic structure on the Forth & Clyde was, until very recently, the Kelvin aqueduct. Construction work was frequently delayed, but when the aqueduct was finally completed in 1790 it was the largest in the country, at 445ft long. The etching by James Hopkirk clearly shows that this was a ship canal, and originally had a water depth of 8ft, sufficient even for large vessels. Imposing as it is, it has been surpassed by the breathtaking Falkirk Wheel, a boat lift linking this canal to the Union Canal. (*Waterways Archive Gloucester*)

As no one contemplated any sort of unified canal system for the country, no one cared very much about what anyone else was doing, and it was designed to take vessels up to 14ft 3in beam, but just 60ft in length. It began by following the Aire valley but then, as the way steepened, the canal climbed at first through single locks, then by a double lock, a three-lock staircase and reached a climax at Bingley, where the canal was lifted 60ft by the famous five-lock staircase. Having climbed out of the Aire valley, the canal now stayed with the contours taking a serpentine course through the hillocks but with 19 miles to the next lock. It didn't, however, reach that far during Longbotham's time as chief engineer. It had only got as far as Skipton when the money ran out. It finally opened throughout in 1816.

Few canals show more clearly just what a boon the new transport system was to the Industrial Revolution. In its passage through the major towns met along the way, the canal is lined with mills. Skipton, for example, was a market town that grew up in the protective shade of its castle, but now it developed a whole new canalside area of mills and back-to-back terraces. And a short branch line was dug alongside the castle that ended in a wharf designed to take stone from nearby quarries. By far the most impressive site is Saltaire. The industrialist Sir Titus Salt built a vast mill complex and an early example of a model town here, named after himself and the river valley. It had a rich variety of amenities – a church,

Brindley was not the only engineer working on canals in Britain in the early days, nor were all built to take narrow boats. One of the most ambitious undertakings was for a canal across the Pennines – the Leeds and Liverpool. It was built to connect the Mersey to the Aire & Calder and to take the barges already in use on those river navigations. The locks took vessels up to 62ft long and 14ft 3in wide. The photograph shows two of the typical Leeds & Liverpool barges, generally known as 'Short Boats' to distinguish them from the narrow boats. They are being loaded with stone at Church Wharf, just outside Accrington. (*Waterways Archive Gloucester*)

a school, library, hospital, almshouses – but no pub. Salt was no teetotaller, but he saw pubs as places where workers could get together and lay plans to get pay rises.

Canal construction seemed to be galloping ahead in Britain in the years following the opening of the Bridgewater, but external events brought the whole process grinding to a halt. Across the Atlantic in 1776 American states declared their independence and France at once allied itself with the infant nation. The resulting War of American Independence had a disastrous effect on British trade: profits slumped and no one wanted to invest in anything, least of all canals. The first phase had ended and when construction restarted after the war, it did so with new men and new ideas.

Elsewhere in Europe there was progress in canal construction during these years. One obvious candidate was the narrow neck of land in the south of Denmark that separated the North Sea from the Baltic. In 1777 work started on improving the tidal River Eider as far as Rendsburg. A lock then gave access to a canal that covered the 32km section as far as Kiel. In 1785 an edict made the canal an open waterway for vessels of every nation, and it brought immense traffic with more than 3,000 vessels a year using it by the middle of

The Leeds & Liverpool Canal rose through the Aire valley from Leeds in a series of locks, culminating in the five-lock staircase at Bingley. Once boats had reached the top of the staircase the crew could relax as they had reached the long summit level and the next locks to start the journey down to the Mersey were 17 miles away. The photograph, taken some time between 1910 and 1920, shows the locks being repaired. It is a rare opportunity to appreciate the full scale of the system. It was clearly taken at a time when safety at work was not an issue. (*Waterways Archive Gloucester*)

the nineteenth century. It was such a valuable waterway that it was replaced by the more modern, far larger Kiel Canal at the end of the century.

France also started an ambitious programme for new canals. One of these was intended to reduce the cost of coal imports from Flanders, now Belgium. It would link the River Scheldt to the Oise and through the latter to the Seine and Paris. The major problem was a high ridge between St. Quentin and Cambrai. The proposal, approved in 1769, was certainly bold. It called for a tunnel of generous proportions, with a width of 6.5m, but it had to be nearly 14km long. Bear in mind that at much the same time Brindley had baulked at creating a tunnel less than half as wide and a sixth as long and you can imagine just how daring this project was. It was so daunting that a more modest start was made with a 3.25m wide pilot tunnel. That had still only reached a length of just under 10km when the money ran out. More than a million livres, roughly 6 million modern euros today, had been spent and it was calculated it would take another 2.6 million livres to complete it. Work was abandoned and a canal link would not re-emerge as a practical proposition for many years.

At the same time as Britain was developing its canal system, new projects were also being brought forward in France. Among them was the Canal de Bourgogne, running as the name suggests through the heart of Burgundy. It was an immense undertaking, 242km long with 189 locks. As the photograph clearly shows, the locks were built to generous dimensions to take vessels such as this barge, converted into a hotel boat. (*Anthony Burton*)

When Louis XIV came to the throne in 1774, he proved to be a great enthusiast for canal construction as a way of moving France into an industrial future. The most promising scheme was to link the Saône and Yonne through Burgundy. This major undertaking had the highest summit level of any French canal at 378m, 189 locks in 242km and a tunnel at Pouilly-en-Auxois that was to be almost 3.5km long. But that lay in the future. The King had hoped for an industrial revolution in France, but what he got was a political revolution instead. As a result, works such as canal construction simply stopped, and the Canal de Bourgogne was not opened until 1832. It remains, however, one of the most attractive of all French canals and today enjoys a thriving tourist trade. Thanks to the huge political upheavals in Europe and across the Atlantic in the latter part of the eighteenth century, few canals of importance were built for many years. When work restarted, new men appeared with fresh ideas about how they should be built and the materials that could be used.

Chapter 6

Canal Mania

Whereas continental Europe was convulsed, first by the French Revolution and then the Napoleonic Wars, Britain returned to canal construction once the Peace of Versailles had recognised American independence and ended the war with that country. Confidence was restored and money was once again available for investment. Speculators liked what they saw with the first generation of canals. Birmingham canal shares had started at £140 in 1767; by 1782 they were selling for £370 and ten years later they had shot up to £1,170. There was a very good reason for this. The Duke of Bridgewater had said that a good canal had 'coal at the heel of it', and that was exactly what this canal had and trade was booming, bringing in a healthy income from tolls. Now speculators thought of canal shares as quick routes to easy fortunes. If they could get in at the beginning of a new scheme, they had a good chance of selling the shares at a profit even before work got really under way. One commentator at the time described how they were prepared 'to sleep in barns and stables, when beds could not be procured at the public houses' so as to be on the spot when a new share issue was available. Another noted that they were even prepared to snap up shares before the Act had passed through Parliament. And in the early 1790s acts were being passed at an incredible rate: eight in 1792, twenty-one in 1793 and twelve in 1794. It is no wonder that these years came to be known as the years of canal mania.

Inevitably some schemes were complete duds that were never going to make a penny. The Oakham Canal is a case in point. Melton Mowbray had already been connected to Leicester and the new canal was to extend navigation to Oakham. It was never altogether clear where the traffic was to come from but the Act was duly passed in 1793. It was hardly a direct route. The modern road between the two towns is just 10 miles long; the canal stretched that to 15 miles. It started off by heading north from Oakham, before turning west towards Melton Mowbray. There was a long diversion around Stapleford Park, the estate of Lord Harborough, as the family did not want transport routes across their land. The canal company deferred to his lordship's wishes. It never showed a profit and after just forty-five years it was bought up by the Midland Railway, which built over part of the route. That was one extreme. At the opposite end of the spectrum were canals such as the Grand Junction that was to form a vital part of a new main line between London and Birmingham and was later incorporated into the highly successful Grand Union Canal. The engineer for the latter was William Jessop, one of the new generation of civil engineers who followed on from Brindley with new ideas and new technology.

William Jessop sketched by George Dance
in 1796, at the height of the canal mania
years. He, more than anyone else, carried
the burden of overseeing canal construction
during the mania years of the 1790s as chief
engineer on many of the most important
projects of the day, both in mainland Britain
and in Ireland. There is one other portrait
of Jessop, still in possession of the family.
Where two other great engineers, Brindley
and Telford, chose to be painted with their
most imposing canal works as a background,
Jessop is shown here as a man of learning,
with a handsome leather-bound volume
at his elbow and indications of a more
considerable library behind him. (*National
Portrait Gallery, London*)

Jessop's father was a shipwright who lived in Stoke Damerel, close to the Devonport dockyard. He was in charge of maintenance on the old wooden Eddystone lighthouse but when that caught fire during a terrible storm in 1755, Jessop joined John Smeaton in building the new, solid stone lighthouse. William was born in 1745 and in 1759 Smeaton took him on as an apprentice. It was the ideal start for a boy who was destined to become a notable engineer. He was soon involved in river navigation schemes, not as an apprentice but as an assistant. By 1772 he was working on his own and signing himself William Jessop, engineer.

His big chance came soon afterwards. Following the success of the Newry Canal, the most important project in Ireland was the Grand Canal, planned to join Dublin to the Shannon. It was on a grand enough scale to justify its name, with locks capable of taking 175 tonne barges. Work had started in 1756 under the engineer Thomas Omer, who was replaced in 1763 by John Trail. By 1770 a great deal of money had been spent, 20 miles had been completed but none of it was open for traffic. In 1771 the authorities decided to call in an outside expert and they approached Smeaton. The engineer agreed to come to Ireland for only one visit, but recommended 'a young Gentleman who has just begun Business for himself, who has served me 13 years, viz. 7 years as an apprentice, and 6 years as an Assistant, and whom I have always found docile and intelligent'. Jessop's fee would be one guinea a day, which was good news for the Company as Smeaton was charging them five guineas, plus a handsome travel allowance. Smeaton recommended a new line and

The Grand Canal of Ireland was proposed in the early eighteenth century, although work did not get under way until the 1750s. Progress was slow until Jessop took over and the whole main line, 82 miles from the Liffey in Dublin to the Shannon, was completed in 1804. Although as with many other canals its once lucrative cargo traffic has ended, it has become a popular tourist route. The canal here is shown passing through the heart of Dublin in what is now a very attractive area and the broad locks, designed to take barges, these days deal with trip boats and holiday makers.

Jessop surveyed the route over the Bog of Allen. At the same time there were problems on another Irish Canal that also needed to be looked at by the English engineers.

The Newry Canal was supposed to cut the cost of coal in Dublin, but the cartage from the mines at Coalisland was higher than the rest of the journey by canal. An extension was supported by the church and promoted by the Archbishop of Armagh, who appointed one of his clergymen, Pastor Johnston, as engineer for the project. He had no experience and struggled with difficult conditions, especially the marshy land near Lough Neagh. In all the annals of canal construction it is doubtful if any canal ever made such slow progress. It was only 4 miles long and had just seven locks, but work that started in 1732 was only completed in 1787. Even then it failed to achieve its objective. There were four mines in the Coalisland area, two of which were easily accessed by the new canal. Unfortunately they were the least productive and the other two were only 3 miles away, but 200ft above the canal. There seemed no obvious solution to the problem, until a French engineer, Daviso de Arcot, a name usually anglicised to Ducart, appeared.

He proposed using small craft, unlike the large barges used on the rest of the canal. They would hold just one tonne each, but could be moved in strings. To overcome the difference in levels, he built three inclines, varying from 55ft to 70ft long. The boats could be lowered on these over rollers. This sounds like the system used on the Grand Canal in China, and it was a system already in use in Europe, which is probably where Ducart got his idea. Smeaton, on his trip to Europe in the 1750s, had seen schemes in the Netherlands, known as 'windlasses', where slopes with rollers moved vessels from one dyke to another at a slightly different level. Ducart had travelled in Europe, looking at canal works there and may have seen such systems.

The Coalisland incline was not a great success as the boats kept sticking, and Jessop recommended using a double track and extending the length of the boats. By 1790, however, according to William Chapman who wrote a treatise on canals, published in 1797, the system had been changed. Now there were two tracks and the boats were floated onto cradles, which was the basis for many inclined planes in the canal age. There is no evidence to confirm this, but Jessop might take the credit for introducing the system to Britain. It was not new as far as Europe was concerned. A similar system had already been built at Fusina near Venice. The Brenta river was separated from the Venetian lagoons by a dam, and the incline had been built to get round it. A horse gin moved the vessels along a railed track. Gins such as this were commonly in use in mines for moving material up and down shafts. The horse, walking a circular track, moved a drum around which the rope was wound.

Over the next few years, Jessop gained more experience as an engineer in his own right on important river improvement schemes, including the Calder & Hebble Navigation. But it was with renewed activity in canal construction that he came into his own. His first major work was the Cromford Canal, authorised in 1789. This joined the Erewash at Langley Mill and was carried through a rich mining area to Cromford where it had its terminus close to Sir Richard Arkwright's pioneering cotton mill. Jessop himself described the area through which the canal was to pass as 'rugged and mountainous', adding that 'it will at first sight strike an observer as very ineligible for such a project'. One can only agree. Although the canal was only 14½ miles long, there were four tunnels, one of which, the Butterley tunnel, was 2,966yd long. There were also two major aqueducts: one over the Amber and the other over the Derwent. As if that was not enough, there were problems with water supply, so three reservoirs were also needed. Faced with so many problems, Jessop planned a composite canal: the section from the Erewash to Butterley tunnel would be a broad canal, capable of taking 14ft beam barges, but the long tunnel would be just 9ft wide and the remainder of the canal to Cromford would be narrow.

The building of the canal brought out one of Jessop's most endearing characteristics. He was the man in charge and if things went wrong, he always accepted full responsibility. He had troubles with both the aqueducts. Part of the Amber aqueduct collapsed and Jessop

Butterley tunnel on the Cromford Canal was 2,996 yards long, and built to unusually small dimensions, just 9ft wide and 8ft high at the crown. There was no towpath and boats had to be legged through, as seen here, by walking the boat along with their feet against the sides of the tunnel. It was built by sinking a total of thirty-three shafts, from which the men could work out in either direction, as well as working inwards from the two ends. The tunnel was literally undermined by a nearby colliery and was severely damaged: by the 1920s it was impassable and was never reopened. (*Waterways Archive Gloucester*)

personally paid for the repairs. Then in 1793 a crack appeared in the Derwent aqueduct and it became clear that the walls were not thick enough, and again Jessop footed the bill. In a technical sense he was to blame, but this was complex engineering work and the budget was never big enough to do a thorough job. He had economised in his use of materials on the aqueducts but had gone too far. Needless to say, the financiers did not consider it was their responsibility. His work on the Cromford Canal may have hurt Jessop's pocket, but it did wonders for his reputation. He was seen both as a good engineer and an honest man. Just as Brindley had been the man everyone wanted to employ in the early years of canal building in Britain, now it was Jessop who was in demand all over the country. He was also about to return to Ireland.

Progress on the Grand Canal was slow. The high ambitions of 137ft by 20ft locks proved impractical and far too expensive; this was later reduced to 80ft by 16ft and then Smeaton recommended an even greater reduction to 60ft by 14ft. Jessop was called in as a consulting engineer at least as early as 1789, since in a letter of 1790 he told the authorities he would be coming over 'for two or three months as formerly'. He eventually standardised all the locks at 63ft by 14ft. The greatest problem he faced was crossing the great peat morass,

The Derwent aqueduct carries the Cromford Canal across the river. It caused trouble in the early years and when cracks appeared in 1793 it had to be reinforced with iron tie bars. The building at the far end of the aqueduct is the Leawood Pumping Station, built in 1849 to bring water up from the River Derwent to feed the canal. The Cornish beam engine is still in there, has been restored to full working order and is regularly steamed by volunteers on open days. This section of the canal, between here and Cromford, is still open. (*Anthony Burton*)

The canals that crossed the Pennines served areas that were developing important textile industries: mainly woollens in Yorkshire and cotton in Lancashire. The Huddersfield Narrow Canal had Britain's longest canal tunnel at 3 miles 135 yards, but it also needed a steady processions of locks: forty-two on the Huddersfield side and thirty-two to Ashton-under-Lyne. The photograph shows the canal between Marsden, at the eastern end of Standedge tunnel, and Huddersfield. With so many locks, reservoirs were essential, and one can be seen to the left of the lock. To the right is the mill pond that served the large woollen mill. The canal was derelict for many years but has now been fully restored. (*Anthony Burton*)

the Bog of Allen. To gain firm enough ground to hold a puddled channel, he had to build drainage ditches to either side, and his experience in drainage work in the English Fens must have come in useful here. It took five years to complete the canal across the bog, but the results were not entirely successful: there were frequent problems with the collapse of the clay banks. It was finally completed in 1804. By this time, Jessop had been at work on major canal schemes in mainland Britain.

The first canal designed to cross the Pennines was the Leeds & Liverpool, already mentioned in Chapter 5, but in the 1790s it was still far from complete. It had avoided the obstacle presented by the range of hills by taking a huge sweeping curve to the north. In 1794 an act was passed for a more direct route, the Rochdale Canal, that would link the Calder & Hebble navigation at Sowerby Bridge with the Bridgewater Canal in Manchester. The first plans had been drawn up by John Rennie. It was to be a canal on a grand scale with locks taking vessels 14ft 2in by 74ft and with an immense 3,000yd long tunnel through the Pennines at the summit. Rennie did not stay with the project and it was passed to Jessop, who wanted nothing to do with creating such a tunnel. Instead his canal was to have ninety-two locks in just 33 miles and was to cross the summit in a deep cutting. With so many locks, and only a short summit level, the biggest problem would be water supply. Jessop put in hand two immense reservoirs at Hollingsworth and Blackstone Edge but a third had later to be added. It is easy to admire the engineering that produced two vast watery staircases spanning the Pennine Hills, but creating the reservoirs was no less impressive. The Hollingsworth reservoir, for example, is contained behind a vast bank, 10ft wide on the top and sloping in a 1:2 ratio to its base. At its heart is a 9ft thick core of puddle clay.

There was to be one other direct route through the Pennines, whose engineer was Benjamin Outram. He became a partner with Jessop. During the building of the Cromford Canal, large iron ore deposits were found and Jessop and Outram formed the Butterley Iron Works to take advantage. Outram, it seems, did not share Jessop's distaste for Pennine tunnels. The Huddersfield Narrow Canal – the name distinguishes it from an earlier broad canal that it joined in Huddersfield – was authorised in 1794. It too was heavily locked: thirty-two on the Lancashire side, forty-two in Yorkshire. In between was Britain's longest tunnel. Standedge tunnel is 3 miles 135 yards long, a narrow opening without the benefit of a towpath. The difficulties in creating this exceptionally long tunnel were immense. Four steam engines had to be erected on the rough moorland above the canal to pump out water during construction. Anyone walking over Standedge Moor today can see the remains of one of the engine houses and the vast heaps of spoil hauled up from the various shafts. The canal finally opened in 1804, held up less by technical difficulties than the company running out of money. As with the Rochdale Canal, the Huddersfield needed reservoirs to serve the long strings of locks. Ten were built high on the moors but the earth banks frequently leaked. In 1799 there was a far more serious breakage in the Tunnel End dam that sent water crashing down the Colne valley at Marsden causing huge damage and halting work on the canal. The company had to go back to Parliament to get a new act to raise extra money to continue the work. Later another reservoir was built on Marsden Moor and on the night of 29 November 1810, the dam wall collapsed. It became known as the Night of the Black Flood. The Colne Valley was again inundated and this time not just property suffered: six people died.

In 1793 Jessop himself was put in charge of the most prestigious canal scheme in Britain – the Grand Junction. It was to form a new, direct link between Birmingham and London, running from a junction with the Oxford Canal at Braunston to the Thames at Brentford, with an additional, lock-free branch to Paddington. Few canals demonstrate the changes that had occurred between the age of Brindley and the new era of men like Jessop. At first the canal from Brentford takes an obvious route following the course of the River Brent. But where earlier engineers might have staggered the locks along the valley, Jessop grouped most of them in a flight of six at Hanwell. The canal climbed steadily to a point more than 300ft above the tidal Thames and there it reached the line of the Chiltern Hills, stretching right across the route.

The canal had been built as a barge canal, taking vessels up to 14ft 3in. This represented a considerable obstacle, since a tunnel would need to be wide enough to accommodate them. There was no question of going over the top, so Jessop opted for a third alternative.

The canal would dive through the hills in a deep cutting at Tring. This was to be a mile and a half long and, at its deepest point, the edge of the cutting would be more than 30ft above the bed of the canal. Nothing on this scale had ever been attempted and one reason that it was practical was a large workforce experienced in canal cutting. They were originally known as navigators, men who dug the navigations, but this was soon shortened to the more familiar navvy. These were specialist workers, with no permanent home, who travelled from canal working to canal working, where their services were needed – and where the best rates were paid. An experienced navvy could shift about twelve cubic yards of earth a day, but even with their prodigious strength it needed an army of men to complete Tring. The work required the men to move more than half a million cubic feet of material, very little of which would be easily worked soft soil. At the height of the construction period, there were some 10,000 navvies at work at Tring.

The Grand Junction Canal, now incorporated as part of the Grand Union Canal, was one of Britain's most successful waterways. It was the major link in a through route, connecting Birmingham and the manufacturing districts of the Midlands to London. Many industrialists built canalside factories to make use of its facilities, both to bring in raw materials and send out finished products. The Ovaltine factory was established at King's Langley in the early twentieth century and ran its own fleet of narrow boats. (*Anthony Burton*)

Deep cuttings called for a new technique. It would have been impossible just to push barrow loads of soil straight up to the top of the cutting, so barrow runs were introduced. These consisted of steep sloping planks laid on trestles up the cutting slopes. Barrows could be pulled up by horses at the top, but the men had to walk up behind the barrows to keep them on the planks. One can imagine what the barrow runs must have been like, covered in wet clay and dirt, and just how easy it would be for a man to lose his footing. If he did, he had to drop the barrow off to one side and throw himself off in the opposite direction to avoid being buried under the heavy spoil. Coming down, he ran down the planks, pulling the empty barrow behind him. There are no known illustrations of canal barrow runs, but a generation later Robert Stephenson built the London & Birmingham Railway. His route closely followed Jessop's and he too opted for a deep cutting at Tring. Contemporary illustrations show the barrow runs, looking much as they must have done in Jessop's day.

The Tring cutting lies at the summit of the canal, so this was an important site. The first essential was to supply it with water, which was originally planned as coming from springs near Wendover. As a channel had to be cut anyway, it was made into not just a conduit but also a navigable arm for the main canal. In time, this proved inadequate and three

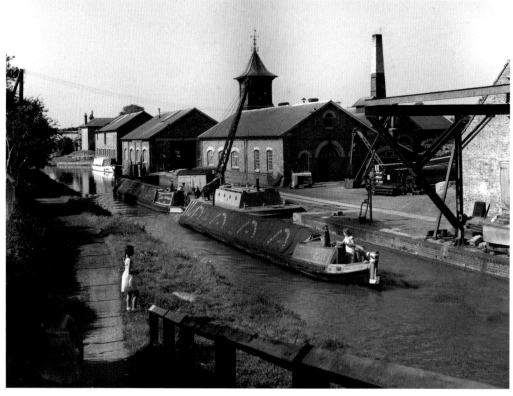

The Grand Junction had its own maintenance yard at Bulbourne at the northern end of the Tring cutting. They produced both wood and ironwork, including new lock gates (see illustration p.30). (*Anthony Burton*)

reservoirs had to be built. With so much going on at this point it seemed sensible to build a maintenance yard here at the northern end of the cut. Bulbourne Yard remains much as it was in Jessop's day, at least externally. Even when one goes inside the building it still has its traditional blacksmith's forge.

Jessop needed to provide aqueducts for the new canal, which we shall look at in the next chapter, but his most difficult task came with the building of two tunnels: the 2,042yd one at Braunston and the even longer 3,056yd Blisworth tunnel. Contractors had failed to meet the standards set by the engineer, but there were difficulties that had not been allowed for. At Braunston, the workers found quicksand that had not appeared in the test borings. Work on Blisworth dragged on for years. These were tunnels on a large scale, wide enough to take either barges or to allow two narrow boats to pass each other. At Blisworth, work was carried out from nineteen shafts as well as from the two ends. Both

One of the most difficult undertakings on the Grand Junction Canal was the construction of the 3,057 yard long Blisworth tunnel. It was built to far more generous dimensions than the Butterley tunnel (p.81), 16ft 6in wide with a crown 11ft above water level. It was lined with brick, but had no towpath, so as at Butterley, boats had to be legged through. Because of the width, the only way men could reach the tunnel sides was to lie on wings – boards projecting on either side of the boat. For many years, professional leggers were employed. By the early twentieth century, when the tunnel had been open for a hundred years, it needed extensive reconstruction. Here, the workers pose for their picture on completion of the work in 1910. It gives a good idea of the size of the tunnel, and the tools the men hold indicate that the work still depended largely on manual labour. (*Waterways Archive Gloucester*)

The Grand Junction Canal entered the Thames at Brentford and boats heading for the Port of London continued the rest of the journey by river. There was also a branch to Paddington. In 1812 work began on an extension of the Paddington Arm, the Regent's Canal that passed through north London to enter the Thames at a new dock complex at Limehouse. It involved building a tunnel at Islington, and this illustration appears to be the only one produced, showing a canal tunnel under construction. In the distance, men work with pickaxes at the face, and the wooden centring for construction of the brick arched roof can be seen just in front of them. A box is being lowered or raised in the shaft. These boxes could be used either to bring down essential material, such as bricks, or to remove spoil. The boxes could be fitted onto simple bogies that were moved along the temporary railed tracks. (*Waterways Archive Gloucester*)

tunnels had to be lined with brick, but this was not an age where you simply ordered the material from a brickyard. They were made on site: the clay was dug, shaped and fired in temporary kilns. The results were not the uniformly shaped and coloured bricks you would find on a modern site. Colours varied enormously, depending on where the bricks had been placed in the firing, and this only adds to the charm of even the simplest of structures on eighteenth-century canals.

Contemporary illustrations of actual canal construction are very rare, but there is one showing work in progress on the Regent's Canal tunnel at Islington. In the distance, one can see workers at the face of the tunnel with pickaxes. Immediately behind them is wooden centring on which the brickwork arch for the tunnel will be formed. In the foreground, a large wooden crate of spoil is being raised up a shaft, while another crate on a four wheeled trolley is being pushed along one of a pair of wooden tracks. The whole scene is lit by a man holding a flare who, like all the others, is stripped to the waist. There is also physical evidence on other canals of how tunnels such as Blisworth were built.

One of the most unusual tunnels is at Dudley on the canal linking the main line of the Birmingham Canal to the Staffs & Worcester. It began in 1775 as Lord Ward's Canal to link the Birmingham Canal to a complex mine system under Castle Hill. It was then extended between 1784 and 1792. In places it opens out to cavernous vaults; in parts it is brick-lined, low and narrow, but in other parts the bare rock is exposed. It is here that you can still see semi-circular grooves in the rock face. These are what remain of holes drilled by hand into the rock, filled with gunpowder that after it exploded left this telltale sign, showing the point where rock has split away.

The Grand Junction opened in 1805 and was an immense success. Not all Jessop's projects are as well known as this, but some demonstrate why the canals of this period were different from their predecessors. The canals of the mania years not only brought in a new generation of engineers but also a change in technology. Where the first canals of the Brindley era had crept across the landscape, squirming round hills and valleys to keep on the level, the second generation of canals had taken a much bolder approach. This can be seen very clearly on what is now a largely abandoned and forgotten waterway – the Barnsley Canal. Although a comparatively short canal, just 11½ miles long, it needed a great deal of engineering work. There are fifteen locks, designed to take barges up to 78ft long and 14ft wide. The canal also had to cope with a high ridge running right across the route, which Jessop carved through in a deep cutting, the spoil of which was then used to build up an embankment that strode across the next valley –the technique of 'cut and fill'.

Jessop was not the only notable engineer at work during the early 1790s. John Rennie's background was different from that of Jessop and even less like that of Brindley. He was

Looking down on the deep cutting on the Barnsley Canal. Scattered along the bank are great blocks of sandstone, giving a good idea of the conditions the engineers faced in constructing the cutting. The stone would be drilled by hand and the holes filled with gunpowder to blast the rocks apart. All the material would then have been cleared away by hand and taken away in carts to build an embankment. (*Museum of London*)

born at Phantassie in Scotland in 1761. His father was a farmer and owner of a brewery. The young Rennie was interested in all things mechanical, and learned the craft of millwright from another remarkable man, Andrew Meikle, inventor of the threshing machine. He combined this practical experience with studying at Edinburgh University. Scottish universities were far ahead of their English counterparts in offering studies in the sciences, and Rennie was scathing of the English system, as his son, Sir John Rennie, himself a distinguished engineer, reported in his autobiography:

'My father wisely determined that I should go through all the graduations, both practical and theoretical, which could not be done if I went to the University, as the practical parts, which he considered most important, must be abandoned: for he said, after a young man has been three or four years at the University of Oxford or Cambridge, he cannot, without much difficulty, turn himself to the practical part of civil engineering.'

Rennie's skill as a millwright brought him to the attention of the famous Birmingham industrialist, Matthew Boulton, who put him in charge of building the immense Albion Corn Mill on the Thames in London. The city saw his greatest triumphs, including work on new docks and the design for three bridges: London, Southwark and Waterloo. Rennie would be astonished that his London Bridge is now a tourist attraction in Arizona.

John Rennie was an engineer known as much for his elegant designs as for his technological abilities. This was shown very clearly on the Kennet & Avon Canal. It began at the western end, joining the navigable Avon at Bath. It passed right through the fashionable Sydney Gardens, where its impact was reduced by running in a cutting, crossed by this delightful iron bridge. (*Anthony Burton*)

The most attractive of all the structures designed by Rennie is the Dundas aqueduct that carries the Kennet & Avon across the Avon. Perhaps the inspiration came from the buildings of nearby Bath, for the theme is purely classical. Pilasters ornament the spaces between the arches, and the whole structure is topped by a deeply dentilled cornice and ornate balustrade. It was built from Bath stone quarried locally, a form of limestone that has a rich, creamy colour and adds immensely to the beauty of the scene. (*Anthony Burton*)

His bridges were widely praised for their elegant design, and the same could be said of his aqueducts. He showed a fine sense of proportion, an understanding of classical architectural language and an awareness that different locations needed very different treatments. This is exemplified in his two finest works: Dundas aqueduct on the Kennet & Avon Canal and the Lune aqueduct on the Lancaster. The former, just 5 miles from the start of the canal in the centre of Bath, is as elegant as anything that city offers. Built of the lovely honey coloured dressed Bath stone it strides over the River Avon in a single arch, with two smaller arches on the land at either side. The structure is ornamented by pilasters between the arches and topped by a deeply dentilled cornice and balustrade. The five-arched aqueduct over the Lune in Lancaster uses a similar classical language but more robustly, and the dark stone, instead of being dressed to a smooth finish, is rough-hewn.

Extensive records have survived of work on the Lune aqueduct and the problems encountered by the builders. Similar stories could probably be written about all the great stone aqueducts built in the country at this time. The engineer on the spot was Archibald Millar, who had already gained considerable experience working with Smeaton in Ireland. The first thing to be done was to settle the key men on the site, including a Mr Exley, Millar's principal assistant. Millar ordered the construction of temporary accommodation and workshops, with a saw pit, carpenter's shop, store room, a kitchen and a room for Exley. The latter was to be floored and have a fireplace, but Millar noted that it was all to be done on 'the most frugal plan'. Exley shared his kitchen with 'the Steam Engine man', which must have been trying as the records show that he was often drunk – one report noted 'he has kept the can to his head for 3 or 4 days'.

The first stage of building involved the construction of coffer dams, watertight wooden enclosures, built up by driving piles into the floor of the river. Once completed, the area contained by the piles could then be pumped dry so that men could work inside it, building the foundations for the piers. The crude pile-driving machines were hand operated. It was hard work and dangerous: one unfortunate man lost three fingers when the ram fell on his hand. The coffer dams were never completely clear of water, no matter how much was pumped out by the steam engine, and the men worked in terrible conditions. This was not an age where employers showed great sympathy for any workforce, but the conditions were so bad that Millar recommended giving the men 'some small sum' daily for drink.

Once the piers had risen above water level, building the arches could begin. The wooden framework was constructed by men under the control of the master carpenter, who was also foreman for the whole site. It was hauled into place above the piers and simple cranes erected to lift the heavy blocks of stone into place. Once the keystone was set in the centre of the arch, the centring could be removed. The whole site was teeming with workers – masons, carpenters and navvies. In summer 1794 there were more than 150 men at the Lune site. By the time the aqueduct was completed in 1796 the construction bill had risen to £48,000, roughly £5 million today, which makes it seem a real bargain. There was comparatively small outlay in capital equipment and labour was cheap – the highest paid worker on site, the foreman, only got about £5,000 a year at today's prices and ordinary workmen a good deal less.

Apart from the aqueducts, Rennie's canals, particularly the Kennet & Avon, are good examples of how canal work was advancing in the 1790s. Like Jessop, Rennie kept his locks grouped in long flights. The canal rose from the Avon in Bath via a flight of seven 14ft-wide locks – later reduced to six when two were amalgamated into one rather frighteningly deep lock. From the top of the flight the canal is lock free for nearly 10 miles. This flight is insignificant compared with the twenty-nine locks at Caen Hill that carry the canal up to Devizes. To conserve water, the locks have side ponds terraced into the hillside beside them that act as individual reservoirs. Even with water-saving devices, there was still a need for extra supplies for the long pound between the top of Bath Locks and Bradford-on-Avon and for the short actual summit. Rennie provided two different solutions to the problem.

By the time the canal had climbed to the first long pound, it was some 50ft above the River Avon. There had been an old watermill at Claverton and Rennie used this site to create a pumping station to lift the river water into the canal. Power was supplied by an immense pair of coupled water wheels, each 15ft 6in diameter and 11ft 6in wide. Through gearing these worked a pair of beam pumps of the type familiar from the steam engines of the day. The system could lift 100,000 gallons an hour. They have long since been replaced by a modern pumping system, but when the new engine failed in 1989, the old pumps ably took over the task, just as they had done nearly two centuries before.

On the other site, Rennie used the latest technology. James Watt had improved on the older Newcomen engines. He no longer relied on air pressure to force a piston down in a cylinder. He still condensed the steam, but now in a separate condenser. The cylinder no longer had to be reheated at every stroke, but could be kept permanently hot, with a closed top and lagging round the perimeter. Instead of air pressure, steam pressure acted on the opposite side of the piston from the vacuum. He had partnered with Matthew Boulton, and a Boulton and Watt engine was installed at Crofton in 1812, one of a pair that lift water from a lake to the summit level. The 1812 engine is now the oldest steam engine in the world, still in its original engine house and still capable of doing the job for which it was built. Claverton shifted 100,000 gallons an hour, whereas Crofton manages 250,000 gallons. In their day, canals such as this were at the forefront of technological development.

The steam engine was at the heart of Britain's Industrial Revolution, no longer used just to pump water from mines, but as the prime mover for mills and factories. Canals played a vital role in supplying the coal that kept them going. But the age was also about new materials, and this branch of technology had a profound effect on how waterways were developed at the end of the eighteenth century and beyond.

Chapter 7

The New Iron Age

A great turning point in the industrial history of the eighteenth century came when Abraham Darby of Coalbrookdale, in Shropshire, made iron using coke as a fuel for his furnace instead of charcoal. It may not sound significant, but it had two dramatic effects. Charcoal has to be made from a limited resource – timber – and the forests of Britain also had to provide wood for all kinds of other uses, especially for building ships. Coal was abundantly available, so there were no longer the same restraints on expanding the industry. The other major difference lay in the sort of iron the different furnaces produced. The older works turned out wrought iron, a very pure form of the metal that, as its name suggests, is malleable. Darby produced cast iron with a higher carbon content. Again the name tells you a lot: it could be cast in moulds to replicate the shape of a wooden pattern.

Following the success of Abraham Darby's smelting of iron ore with coke instead of charcoal, new ironworks were developed in the regions where ore and coal were both readily available. One important site, the extensive remains of which can still be seen, was at Blaenavon in South Wales. The illustration shows the rows of furnaces, with the casting houses at the foot. The works were connected via a tramway to the Brecon & Abergavenny Canal. From there, the pig iron could be taken via a direct end-to-end connection down the Monmouthshire Canal to Newport for transhipment.

It also has very different characteristics from wrought iron: the former is very strong in tension, but buckles under pressure; the latter is strong in compression, but cannot be bent without fracturing. The two forms of the metal are both useful, but in very different ways.

At first, the Darby works specialised in making cooking pots, but gradually they extended the use of iron to construction. It was Abraham Darby III who designed the famous bridge across the Severn that gives the town of Ironbridge its name. Opened in 1777, it is a curious structure. Nothing like it had ever been attempted, so it was designed by treating the iron elements that went into its construction as if they were timber. So the bridge is a complex mixture of curved iron segments, either passing through each other or joined by what are, in effect, woodworking joints. It was essentially a one-off, but it was the starting point for a new age of bridge building that spread to the canal world.

On all the early canals, fixed bridges had been built of either brick or stone, depending on the material most readily available close to the working site. When money was running short, engineers would cut costs by using moveable bridges. The simplest type, seen for example on the Oxford Canal, consists of wooden platforms, moved by means of a long balance beam – rather like a lock gate laid on its side. The more complex versions have a superstructure, with a horizontal balance beam at the top that could be pulled down by a chain. This type of bridge is common on Dutch canals and is on some British canals, such as the Ellesmere. The alternative was the more sophisticated swing bridge. Moveable bridges were satisfactory when they were merely carrying tracks, for example where a canal cut off one part of a farmer's land from the rest. They suited the farmer, but boat crews had to stop and open and close them. Mostly, they were simple arches, striding across canal and towpath, providing a hump for the road or track up above. Occasionally, they had to be more complex, for example where the towpath changed sides. As the horse

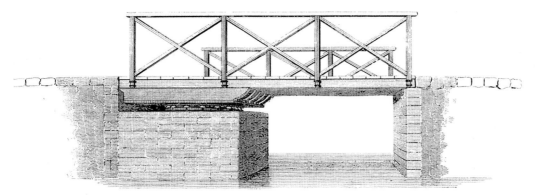

Many canals had moveable bridges, largely because they were cheaper to install than conventional bridges of brick or stone – although maintenance costs were always higher. The most common type were the swing bridges, such as this designed by Thomas Telford. The mechanism is straightforward, the platform being pivoted at one end above a turntable. What is not shown is a balance beam to allow it to be moved, much as the beams are used to open and close lock gates. (*Hugh McKnight*)

A rather more complex bridge is the lift bridge. This example is on the Ellesmere Canal, now generally known as the Llangollen Canal, at Whixall. The superstructure supports a balance beam, one end of which is connected to the platform of the bridge, and the other end has a dangling chain that can be pulled for lifting. This type of bridge was common in Holland long before it came into use in Britain. (*Anthony Burton*)

could not simply cross a conventional bridge, dragging a boat behind it, an alternative design was needed. The simplest structures had long ramps up from the towpath and then equally long ramps leading back on the opposite side in the same direction. This allowed the towrope to pass safely under the arch. More sophisticated versions were used on the Macclesfield Canal, where the towpath curls under the bridge – earning them the name of 'snake bridges'. Conventional bridges depend on the complete arch being in place, but with iron you could make a bridge with a gap in the middle, by building two cantilevered sections that don't meet. The towrope can pass through the gap as the horse walks across the bridge. Examples can be seen on the Stratford Canal.

Cast iron also offered a new option for conventional bridges. Canals are generally designed to be the same width throughout their length, which means that bridges can all be the same design and dimensions. Jessop designed standard conventional bridges for the Grand Junction, building them in brick or stone, depending on the best material available locally, but others recognised that standardisation was perfect for iron. Once you have created a pattern, it can be used over and over again to produce a set of identical components.

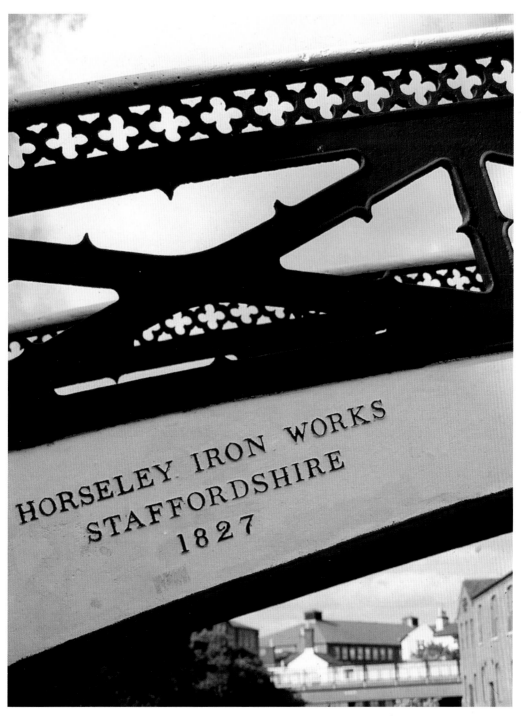

In 1704 the Horseley Iron Works was established on a branch of the Birmingham Canal. The development of the Birmingham system into what became known collectively as the Birmingham Canal Navigations (BCN) required the construction of many new bridges. As the canals were of a uniform width it was possible to cast the parts for what became standardised bridges that could be assembled on site. This example is in Birmingham near the top of the Farmer's Bridge flight of locks. (*Anthony Burton*)

One of the problems canal engineers faced was building a bridge at a point where the towpath changed from one side of the canal to the other – a turnover bridge. The options were at first limited. The boatmen could be made to unhitch the tow rope, lead the horse over the bridge and reattach the rope on the other side, or a bridge could be built with a complex of ramps going up one side, and turning back under the arch on the other. With cast iron, the job became simpler. You could make a bridge that would be in effect a pair of cantilevers with a small gap between them, through which the rope could be passed. This example is on the Stratford-on-Avon Canal at Lapworth. (*Anthony Burton*)

One company in particular is associated with producing standardised cast-iron bridges for Midlands canals. The Horseley Iron Works had its foundry on a branch off the Birmingham Canal and many of its bridges were designed for the complex of canals in that region known as the Birmingham Canal Navigations (the BCN). The bridge is cast in sections. Each side section consists of a flat arch with integral handrail. The two sides can then be linked by locking plates, above which smaller iron plates are laid to create the roadway. They are simple but elegant. Not all iron bridges came in standard sizes. When Thomas Telford was appointed to improve the canal system in Birmingham, he realised that Brindley's old wandering line needed to be replaced by a more direct route. This involved, in places, carving through the rising ground that the older engineer had avoided. One of these deep cuttings needed to be crossed by a high-level bridge, and a very handsome arch was built to carry the roadway. Known as Galton Bridge, it demonstrated how far design had come since Darby's day. No one any longer thought of iron as simply a replacement for timber, but recognised that it called for new construction methods. The main 150ft span arch comprises six ribs, each consisting of seven segments bolted together.

These are joined to the roadway above by a lattice of diagonal struts. Iron could also solve the problem of turnover bridges.

A far more daring use of iron appeared in 1787 on the Severn at Ironbridge. In the middle of the sixteenth century, a strange woman, known as Mother Shipton, lived in a riverside cave in Knaresborough, Yorkshire. She gathered her prophecies in a poem that included the lines:

'On water iron then shall float
As easy as a wooden boat.'

Because of outlandish ideas such as this she was generally thought mad. 'Mad' was also applied to John Wilkinson, not in the sense that he was deranged but because he was besotted with using iron in previously unthought of ways – he even had his own iron coffin propped up in a corner of his office. 'Iron Mad' Wilkinson made Old Mother

The Horseley works not only provided bridges in Birmingham. To improve communications between the northern end of the Grand Junction Canal at Braunston and Birmingham, it was decided to improve the next section of the route along the northern section of the Oxford canal. This was a typically wandering Brindley canal and it was decided to create a new, straighter route. This wintry scene shows one of the new bridges near Newbold-on-Avon. It displays how the Horseley bridges were assembled: the main structure consists of a pair of iron arches, which are then joined together by metal plates to form the roadway. (*Anthony Burton*)

Shipton's prophecies a reality. He built an iron barge, *The Trial*, that launched on the Severn at Coalbrookdale in July 1787. 'It answers all my expectations', he wrote, 'and it has convinced the unbelievers, who were 999 in a thousand'. Iron boats were particularly useful for tub-boat canals, variations on the theme we saw developed at Coalisland.

Another iron master, William Reynolds, who was anxious to join his works to the River Severn, further developed improved ways for using inclined planes for canals in very hilly country. He needed large supplies of ironstone and coal for his foundry at Ketley. These were available just a mile and a half away and could be brought by canal, but at the end there was a 73ft drop. It would have been impossible to build locks, as there was no adequate water supply. Instead he built an inclined plane. This consisted of two parallel sets of iron rails leading down the slope. The little tub boat would be floated into a lock, which was then drained, the water passing into a reservoir, from which it could be pumped back by steam engine. As the water level dropped, the boat settled on a carriage, with different sized wheels to keep it level. The carriage was fastened by chains that passed round a drum to connect with a second carriage on the opposite track. As the cargo was only moving down the slope, the weight would be sufficient to haul the empty boat back from the bottom. Completed in 1787, the system worked well as Reynolds wrote in a letter to James

The most splendid iron bridge across a canal was designed by Thomas Telford when he was chief engineer developing the new main line for the Birmingham Canal. Galton Street Bridge crosses the canal, at a point where it lies in a deep cutting, in a single, elegant arch. Sadly, although the bridge still exists, this open view has been lost. A new road bridge has been built at a lower level and the canal passes under it in a tunnel that is basically a concrete tube. (*Waterways Archive Gloucester*)

The Double Inclined Plane

This illustration shows one particular type of inclined plane. The double track carries two tub boats, so that there is a counterbalancing effect. The boats are moved by means of chains and the motive power comes from the weight of a large bucket full of water dropping down the well to the right of the framework. When the bucket reaches the bottom, a valve connects with a projection to empty the water. A boat going down the slope would then raise the bucket again. One of the most impressive uses of this system was on the Bude Canal. This was mainly used to bring beach sand inland for fertilising and had a series of inclines. The largest, which was worked in this way, was at Hobbacott Down: it was 995ft long and raised the boats by a vertical height of 220ft. (*Bodleian Library, University of Oxford*)

Watt. He said it had met his 'most sanguine expectations … we have already let down more than forty boats per day each carrying 8 tons … and have not yet had an accident'.

This was just the first of many inclined planes built in the area. The Shropshire Canal was authorised in 1788, a modest affair in length at 7½ miles long, but the country was seemingly impossible for conventional canal technology. The summit of this short waterway would be more than 300ft above the river. Once again the answer was found with inclined planes. There were three: the first, the Hay incline, lifted the boats for 207ft from the Severn at Coalport; the next was a lift of a further 126ft to the summit; and a third dropped the canal by 120ft to join the Donnington Wood Canal. Few traces remain of the pioneering Ketley incline, but the Hay incline has not only survived but also been restored as part of the Ironbridge Museum site at Blists Hill. Parts of the canal are in water and one can also see the simple iron tub boats that were used. The Trench Incline on the old Shrewsbury Canal was the last to remain in use, only going out of service in 1921, which meant it survived long enough to be photographed in its working days.

Inclined planes also found a use in the West Country, notably on the Bude Canal. The main reason for building the canal was to carry the sand from Bude on the coast, inland to

The Trench inclined plane on the Shrewsbury Canal, photographed c.1900. The wooden tub boat has been floated onto the carriage. On this incline the power is supplied by a steam engine housed at the top of the incline. (*Waterways Archive Gloucester*)

the farms of Cornwall. The sand was largely composed of shells, so had a very high calcium content and could be used instead of lime as a fertiliser. This was a huge trade – records show 4,000 cart loads of sand being removed in a single day. The entrance to the canal is through a sea lock, then the canal follows the line of the river, until it meets the hills that stand between it and the upland farms. The answer lay with inclines and the site of the first, the Hobbacott Down incline, can still be traced. It was immense, 935ft long and rising 225ft, and the working of the incline was described in a travel handbook published in 1865. The system was rather different from that of the Shropshire inclines. On the Bude Canal, the barges themselves were fitted with wheels. The rails dipped into the water, the wheels were set in place and a chain attached. At the top of the incline was a massive bucket filled with water that was attached to the opposite end of the chain fastened to the boat. The bucket then dropped down a deep well, dragging the boat up the slope. When the bucket hit the bottom, a plug in the bucket connected with a stake, opening a valve to release the water. There were two tracks, and the empty bucket was connected to another in a second well, so that as one descended the other was raised. There was a steam engine on hand, but was only used where necessary. This effective technology once again had its origins in the work of iron masters.

Many structures associated with canals and rivers benefitted from the new technology. Jessop's early work on the Albion Mill in London went up in flames in a fire, and such accidents were all too common in buildings that relied on wooden pillars and beams. By the end of the eighteenth century, buildings with a cast-iron frame were common. And the iron was not only used structurally. Many canalside warehouses have standardised cast-iron window frames. The material even made its way into a broadsheet ballad of the period:

Canals were generally required to provide mileposts along the route. Originally they would have been individually carved from stone blocks, but with cast iron a standard design could be made, and only small adjustments to the numbers were needed between castings. This milepost stands at the junction of the Montgomery and Ellesmere Canals. (*Anthony Burton*)

'Since cast-iron has got all the rage,
And scarce anything's now made without it;
As I live in this cast-iron age,
I mean to say something about it.
There's cast-iron coffins and carts,
There's cast-iron bridges and boats,
Corn-factors with cast-iron hearts,
That I'd hang up in cast-iron coats.'

By far the most dramatic use of iron in the canal story comes with the building of aqueducts. To find out how it began we have to turn back to William Jessop and his busy life and commitments.

During the mania years of the 1790s, the demands on Jessop were extreme. Just like Brindley before him, he was the man of the moment and all the scheme promoters wanted him. Although he could do the initial work on a number of canals, he could not give all of them his full attention: he needed to establish priorities and a reliable man to act in his place. One canal on which he was the chief engineer was the Ellesmere. It had its origins in the need to make a useful connection with the existing Chester Canal. This had been built to run south from Chester to end at a point near Nantwich and, without extra connections, it served no obvious purpose. What was needed was a link to an area that would provide trade. The selected area was North Wales, with its mines and ironworks, together with an extension northwards to the Mersey. It took its name from the little market town along the route and it is doubtful if Jessop considered this his most important commission. He had hoped to appoint a trusted assistant, William Turner, to the post but he was overruled by the Committee of Proprietors who wanted the job to go to their own man, even though he had no experience in canal work. His name was Thomas Telford.

Telford was born in Eskdale in the Southern Upland hills of Scotland in 1757. His father, a shepherd, died when he was an infant and his mother had to leave the cottage where he was born to settle in a single room with the baby. It was not a promising start, but Telford acquired an education and, thanks to a local lady, Elizabeth Pasley, he took an interest in literature. In later life he claimed that the first book that enthralled him was Milton's *Paradise Lost*, scarcely typical reading for a teenager of any generation. Schooling was necessarily brief, for the family were desperate for money. He was apprenticed to a local stonemason and learned his craft well. But he was ambitious and knew he could never prosper if he remained in rural Eskdale. His first foray away from home took him to Edinburgh, where great building works were in progress, with the construction of the New Town in the shadow of the castle. It was not long, however, before he headed for London, where he got engaged on one of the most prestigious projects of the day – Somerset House. His natural talents were considerable and in his spare time he studied all kinds of subjects – in one letter to a friend in Scotland he declared himself 'deep in Chemistry'. He was clearly no ordinary stonemason.

His gifts were recognised by the newly appointed MP for Shrewsbury, William Pulteney. He planned to make a new residence for himself in the dilapidated Shrewsbury Castle, and invited Telford to Shropshire to look after the restoration. It was a decisive moment for he was soon offered an even more prestigious position as county surveyor for Shropshire. The post offered all kinds of opportunity, including the building of the first of many bridges he designed over the years, this one crossing the Severn at Montford. He also tried architecture, designing two churches at Bridgnorth and Madeley. He even became involved in archaeology with excavations at the Roman town of Wroxeter. He had established himself in the area as an intelligent man and capable of working in different disciplines. The main subscribers to the Ellesmere Canal were Shropshire men and they insisted their protégé got the job.

Jessop had planned the canal with his usual care, using contour cutting where appropriate and driving a straight line where that represented the ideal solution. He had ensured water supplies by building a weir across the River Dee near Llangollen to feed the main canal through a narrow, but navigable, branch. Because Llangollen is now seen as the end of

The Longdon aqueduct carried the now derelict Shrewsbury Canal over the little River Tern. It represents a pioneering use of the iron trough and is a comparatively simple structure, with the triangular iron supports set into stone blocks. The towpath is outside the water-filled trough. The light iron trough contrasts with the bulky stone abutments that were built for what was meant to be a conventional masonry canal. Designed by Thomas Telford and the ironmaster William Reynolds, it was one of two aqueducts that were the first to use an iron trough, the other being Benjamin Outram's structure on the Derby Canal. The latter was demolished, and although it was carefully dismantled with a view to preservation, the parts were lost. (*Anthony Burton*)

the navigable canal, it is generally known by that name today. Problems included crossing marshy land at Whixall Moss, but that probably seemed a minor inconvenience to the man who had struggled with the Bog of Allen. The biggest obstacle was how to cross the River Dee, which ran at a level far below that of the canal. The most promising idea was to build locks down either side of the valley to reduce the height above the river and the length between the banks. This could then be bridged by a conventional aqueduct. There was, of course, a problem. With water coming down both sides, the aqueduct would act as a sump, and a pumping system would have had to be introduced to return water to the higher levels. But before this could be tackled, Telford was called away on another task.

Work had already begun on the Shrewsbury Canal, a modest waterway just 18 miles long, when the engineer, Josiah Clowes, died suddenly, leaving it unfinished. The one engineering work of note was an aqueduct over the River Tern at Longden. The river was not navigable so a typical low masonry structure was planned. Work had actually begun when a flood carried away much of the unfinished masonry. The obvious next step was simply to rebuild it as originally designed, but the chief promoter of the canal was the iron master William Reynolds. He was always looking for new ideas and for new ways of using the iron he manufactured. He and Telford came up with a radical new proposal: they would rebuild the aqueduct with an iron trough. The existing stone abutments were cut back, and the 187ft gap closed with the trough, consisting of twenty-six sections bolted together. An iron walkway on the outside of the trough acted as a towpath for the horses. The advantages of the system were obvious: the ironwork was much lighter than masonry and there was no need to line it with puddle clay. The other iron-trough aqueduct designed at that time was on the Derby Canal, designed by Jessop's partner, Benjamin Outram.

Telford now realised that this new type of structure offered a far more elegant solution to the problem of the Dee crossing on the Ellesmere Canal. In March 1795 he proposed an iron aqueduct that could be built at the height of the canal and so would not require either locks or expensive pumps. The plan was accepted and the result was the most spectacular canal aqueduct ever built – Pontcysyllte. The structure would be 1,007ft long and 120ft above the River Dee. The trough was to be carried on eighteen piers that were built solid at the bottom, and hollow with cross-bracing nearer the top. The ironwork was provided by the nearby Plas Kynaston ironworks. The trough itself was made out of a complex of metal plates bolted together. Where at Longden the towpath was set outside the trough, here it is cantilevered out over the water, allowing a free flow underneath, while the narrow boats fit snugly between the opposite side and the path. Crossing the great aqueduct is an interesting experience, particularly for the steerer standing at the back, unable to see the edge of the trough. It is the nearest you can get to the sensation of flying in a canal boat.

There has been controversy over who should take the credit for Pontcysyllte. Traditionally the credit belongs to the chief engineer on the project, in this case Jessop. He certainly showed a continued interest in cast-iron aqueducts, including the impressive

Following the success of the Longdon aqueduct, Telford proposed an iron-trough aqueduct as the best solution for carrying the Ellesmere Canal across the deep, wide Dee valley near Llangollen. Jessop, chief engineer for the canal, accepted the suggestion and the result is Pontcysyllte, arguably the most famous structure on the British canal system, which has now been awarded World Heritage status. The photograph shows the central section, rising an imposing 120ft above the River Dee. (*Anthony Burton*)

Iron Trunk that carried the Grand Junction across the Great Ouse. But the idea originated with Telford and was executed under his control. It is safest to share the honours, but contemporaries shower praise on Telford, and it did wonders for his reputation. He went on to be chief engineer in his own right on many important projects. One of these canals, the Birmingham and Liverpool Junction, begun in 1826, also features cast-iron aqueducts, but is notable for the almost aggressively straight line it takes, using the modern technique of 'cut and fill'. Very deep cuttings were made through the hills, and the spoil used to build up equally imposing embankments in the valleys.

It might seem that building up a bank would be easier than digging a cutting, but on the Birmingham and Liverpool Junction the banks caused the greatest problem. This was especially true at Shelmore where the bank stretched for a full mile above the surrounding fields. At the beginning of 1831, there were between 300 and 400 men at work on the site, and 70 horses were kept busy bringing the soil to the site. In Telford's own words, 'the rich marl of which this mound is composed was crushed and dissolved by its own weight, which in some places squeezed out the sides to a considerable extent.' He was convinced drier soil would solve the problem, but a year later the bank was still slipping. Telford was now elderly, and he suggested a new engineer, William Cubitt, should take over. Cubitt diagnosed a different cause: the soil at the bottom was too weak, so when more earth was piled on top it simply gave way. He put even heavier soil on top, hoping this would force out the weaker material and produce a more solid structure. Nothing, however, seemed to work. The work was holding up the opening of the canal, but all Cubitt could say was that the completion date 'has hitherto defied all our calculations'. It took four years to complete and stabilise the great bank.

More than seventy years had gone by since Brindley began his career as a canal engineer. Now one of his greatest successors at the end of his life was still struggling to complete a canal, albeit one built to a very different pattern. And the technology had scarcely changed: it still relied on men armed with nothing more sophisticated than pickaxe and spade. There was, however, one new addition to the canal landscape that came out of this network of canals. When the Ellesmere had been extended north of Chester to reach the Mersey, the important junction between canal and river involved a transhipment point between barges and narrow boats. As at other similar junctions the site was developed as a new town, Ellesmere Port. Here Telford designed a large basin, surrounded by warehouses, built to the very latest design on iron frames, with arched entrances at water level that allowed boats under the buildings for loading and unloading. Much of the complex was destroyed in a twentieth-century fire, but enough remains to give some idea of the scale. The site now houses an important canal boat museum.

The Birmingham and Liverpool Junction Canal marked the end of narrow canal construction in Britain, but canals on a far larger scale had already been built both here and in other European countries.

Chapter 8

The First Ship Canals

The idea of ship canals was not new in the late eighteenth century: the Exeter Ship Canal and the Canal du Midi are early examples. The idea had, however, not been developed again for some time. Telford had a hand in three such canals: two in Britain and one in Sweden. They were canals on a large scale and introduced mechanisation into the construction process.

The first of the trio began life as the Gloucester & Berkeley Canal with an Act of 1793. It was intended to bypass shoals and shallows on the River Severn to allow the largest vessels of the day, up to 15ft draft (later extended to 18ft), to carry on from Berkeley Pill to Gloucester. In spite of the dimensions of the canal, it should have been straightforward, running through largely flat country, with the only locks being those needed to join the canal to the river at either end. The chief engineer was Robert Mylne who, like many in his position, spent little time on the site, entrusting the work to juniors and experienced contractors. But it all went wrong from the start. The man on the spot was Dennis Edson, whose track record was less than inspiring: worked on two canals, dismissed from two canals. For a canal of these dimensions, a huge amount of earth would need to be excavated, so a major contractor should have been involved: the man who got the job had to borrow planks from the parent company. Edson lasted just nine months and was replaced by 26-year-old James Dadford.

A newly developed excavating machine was brought in to speed things up. It was powered by steam and worked something like the now familiar bucket dredger in which a continuous chain of buckets scooped up the earth. It could remove 1,400 barrow loads of spoil in a twelve-hour working day. We know little more about the machine, but all the evidence suggests it was not a success. By 1799, the canal, which had been started at the Gloucester end, had only reached Hardwicke a mere 5 miles away and the cash had run out. The project was stopped and all but forgotten until 1817. That year the Poor Employment Act was passed by Parliament, authorising the government to spend money on public works to help the unemployed. The canal was one of the beneficiaries.

Telford was called in to advise and a new southern terminus was fixed on at Sharpness Point. The comedy of errors, however, continued. The new resident engineer was John Woodhouse whose work did not survive Telford's scrutiny. He had paid an exorbitant price for building stone for the works, which might have been excusable if he hadn't

Originally known as the Gloucester & Berkeley Canal, later changed to the Gloucester & Sharpness, the waterway was intended to take high-masted sailing ships. As a result, there are no fixed bridges on the canal, just a series of swing bridges. In this photograph, the bridge has been opened to allow a tug to pass. The bridge keepers were given little houses to live in, which looked grand with the addition of a classical portico. (*Anthony Burton*)

bought it from his own son. Finally, the competent Thomas Fletcher was brought in and with a big contractor, Hugh McIntosh, on the job, the canal was finally completed in 1827 – it had taken more than thirty years for a canal that was 16¾ miles long. There was one more farcical event before traffic moved on the waterway. Some local lads livened up the opening ceremony by firing an ancient cannon in salute: the whole thing blew to smithereens. Once completed, however, the canal was a great success, able to take ships 150ft long and 22ft beam.

The main features along the canal are the sixteen swing bridges, each of which had a bridge keeper, who lived in a little cottage next to his work. These are curious buildings, small but given an air of grandeur by elaborate porticos at the front. The docks at both Gloucester and Sharpness developed into impressive complexes with great ranges of warehouses. Sharpness became so important that in 1871 the basin was enlarged and a new ship lock was built to take vessels up to 320ft by 60ft. The canal had achieved exactly what its promoters had hoped for. It brought extra trade and prosperity to the River Severn and commercial traffic still travels as far as the basin at Sharpness. The same could not be claimed for the next canal.

A large dock complex was developed at Gloucester, with ranges of imposing warehouses. Sailing cargo ships were still using the docks as recently as the 1920s when this photograph was taken. Today commercial traffic has ceased and the dock area has been redeveloped as a shopping complex, but is also home to a waterways museum. (*Waterways Archive Gloucester*)

As at the northern end of the Gloucester & Sharpness, so at the southern end at Sharpness, where the canal joins the tidal Severn, extensive development has continued since the canal was built. Unlike Gloucester, Sharpness still enjoys commercial traffic. The vessel in the dock has arrived with a cargo of timber from Scandinavia. (*Anthony Burton*)

It began in 1801 with a letter to Thomas Telford from Nicholas Vansittart of the Treasury, asking him to go to Scotland to rescue the local fishing industry. This was only part of the problem facing a country ravaged as recently as the 1740s by civil war and the attempt to restore the Stuart monarchy. The Highlanders' wretched existence was made worse by the Highland Clearances that were removing crofters from the land to make way for sheep farming on large estates, mostly with absentee landlords. Telford reported that the industry needed new, modern harbours but the country was also suffering from poor communications. He suggested building harbours and roads – and also a new canal. These schemes would not just improve transport but also provide much needed jobs for the impoverished Highlanders.

The proposed canal, called the Caledonian Canal, would cut across Scotland from coast to coast and allow vessels to avoid the long and often dangerous passage round the north coast. It would be a ship canal, able to take the largest fishing boats then in use. The idea was to finance it with government funds, if it could be convinced it was worth the effort. Telford's argument was that poverty was forcing families to leave the country to settle overseas, especially in Canada. Three thousand had left in the year of his survey and he

The Caledonian Canal was part of a wider scheme for economic renewal of the Scottish Highlands, which also included road building and harbour construction. Telford came on regular inspections of all the works. This sketch shows him being driven in a gig to the canal workings. An important part of the scheme was to provide employment for the Highlanders, who can also be seen at work. (*A. D. Cameron*)

wrote: 'I am reliably informed three times that number are preparing to leave in the present year.' The government agreed and officially approved the Caledonian in 1803.

There is an obvious route for a canal across Scotland. It would join Fort William to Inverness. Loch Linnhe bites deep into the coast to the west, the Moray Firth to the east. In between is a natural fault line, where Ice Age glaciers have carved out the deep hollow of the Great Glen. Stretched along its length is a string of lochs: Lochy, Oich and Ness. These natural waterways could be stitched together by the artificial canal to form the through route from coast to coast. Jessop was also involved in the detailed planning, and as the reports were signed by both men it is difficult to determine who took the leading role. Jessop was the senior of the two, but Telford had spent more time going over the ground. Whoever was responsible, the plans were for a canal on a most impressive scale. Although originally planned with the fishing industry in mind, war had once again broken out with Napoleonic France, and now it needed to take naval vessels as well. Locks were now designed to be 170ft by 40ft and the canal was broadened to 100ft. This was going to need engineering works on an unprecedented scale.

Telford faced a problem from the start. By now, British canal constructors were relying on the hardened, tough professional navvies for the toughest tasks, but Telford was committed to using local labour, and most of the Highlanders who came to the works were often both inexperienced and undernourished. A few Scots had already done canal work in England, and Telford hoped they would 'prove useful examples to others'. But there was no great incentive for experienced navvies to travel to the Highlands. In England the going rate was 2s 6d per day (roughly £10 per day today) but on the Caledonian they were only getting 1s 6d (£6.50). Nevertheless, there was no shortage of men desperate for employment. But, unlike on earlier canals, Telford did not have to rely on muscle power alone: machinery helped, and we have a more detailed account of how the works seemed than for any other canal of the age. Telford submitted annual reports to the funding body, and there is also an eye-witness account of what the workings looked like at their busiest time. This is thanks to Telford's friend, the poet Robert Southey, who was given a tour of all the main sites and wrote detailed notes on what he found. Machinery was needed simply because of the difficulties that had to be overcome.

Sea locks had to be built at either end to allow vessels to enter the canal at high tide. The work was begun at the western end, where the lock chamber had to be cut out of solid rock that had to be excavated using hand drills to bore holes for black powder. A coffer dam was built by driving iron piles into the seabed, and the space was kept clear of water by means of a Boulton and Watt steam engine. For more than two months, 200 men worked on the site. Completing the sea lock was only the start of the problems. The River Lochy had to be diverted into a new channel to allow the canal to reach Loch Lochy. But before that point the canal had to be brought over rising ground, first by a double lock and then by a great staircase of eight interconnected locks lifting the canal by 64ft. The ironwork for the

The most prominent feature at the western end of the canal is the set of interconnected locks, known as Neptune's Staircase. In this photograph, taken in the early twentieth century, the locks were still manually operated. To open and close the lock gates, the pairs of poles seen sticking up in the air were inserted into capstans. (*Waterways Archive Gloucester*)

The Caledonian Canal never achieved one of its main objectives – to provide a safe passage for naval vessels between the Irish Sea and the North Sea. It did, however, prove useful for the fishing fleets that followed the shoals of herring and allowed them to avoid the long and difficult journey round the north coast. Here the boats are lined up along the eastern end of the canal at Clachnaharry. (*Waterways Archive Gloucester*)

massive gates was shipped all the way round the coast from Derbyshire and when the locks were completed the gates themselves were opened by a team of men working capstans. We don't have figures for how much the original gates weighed, but the current gates are 22 tonnes each.

Two more locks were needed to take the canal up to the level of Loch Lochy, but at the far end of the loch an even greater obstacle had to be overcome. Only a narrow strip of land separates this loch from the next, Loch Oich, but it rises steeply. It was decided to carve through it in a deep cutting at Laggan. This was one of the busiest spots on the canal during the construction period. The hundreds of men who worked here lived in rough encampments amid ramshackle timber stores and temporary homes for the overseers. By this time there were well over a thousand men at work on different parts of the canal, and provisions was a major problem. The company provided oatmeal at what was described as 'prime cost' and at one site, a brewery was installed, with the optimistic hope, in Telford's own words, 'that the workmen may be induced to relinquish the pernicious habit of drinking whisky.' Southey described the scene at Laggan from his journal of 1819:

Today the Caledonian Canal is used almost exclusively by pleasure boats. Yachts cram into the locks at Fort Augustus. The five-lock staircase joins the artificial canal to Loch Ness. The capstans seen in the earlier photograph have long been disused and the lock gates have all been mechanised. (*Anthony Burton*)

'Here the excavations are what they call at "deep cutting", this being the highest ground on the line, the Oich flowing to the East the Lochy to the Western Sea. This part is performed under contract by Mr. Wilson, a Cumberland man from Dalston, under the superintendence of Mr. Easton, the resident engineer. And here also a Lock is building. The earth is removed by horses walking along the bench of the Canal, and drawing laden cartlets up one inclined plane, while the emptied ones, which are connected with them by a chain passing over pullies, are let down another. This was going on in numberless places and such a mess of earth had been thrown up on both sides along the whole line, that the men appeared in the proportion of emmets to an ant-hill, amid their own work. The hour of rest for men and horses is announced by blowing a horn; and so well have the horses learnt to measure time by their own exertions and sense of fatigue, that if the signal be delayed five minutes, they stop of their own accord, without it.'

This was a more sophisticated system than the barrow runs common on other sites. The cutting ends at Loch Oich, but even here work was needed to deepen the lock, as Southey noted:

'At this (the Eastern) end of Loch Oich a dredging machine is employed and brings up 800 tons a day. Mr. Hughes who contracts for the digging and deepening, has made great improvements in this machine. We went on board, and saw the works; but I did not remain long below in a place where the temperature was higher than that of a hot house, and where machinery was moving up and down with tremendous force, some of it in boiling water.'

The next section of canal was mostly straightforward, although Southey described a few difficulties:

'The Oich has, like the Ness, been turned out of its course to make way for the Canal. About two miles from Fort Augustus is Kytra Lock built upon the only piece of rock which has been found in this part of the cutting – and that piece just long enough for its purpose, and no longer. Unless rock is found for the foundation of a lock, an inverted arch of masonry must be formed at very great expence, which after all is less secure than the natural bottom.'

Southey also described how, at Fort Augustus, the canal plunges to Loch Ness in a spectacular staircase:

The two great staircases are the most obviously imposing feature of the Caledonian Canal. In engineering terms, the greatest challenge was creating the deep cutting at Laggan, carved through the narrow neck of land separating Loch Oich from Loch Lochy. It is difficult now to see the scale of the operations, as the banks are overgrown with trees, but some idea can be judged by the way in which the banks seem to dwarf the cabin cruiser. (*Anthony Burton*)

'Went before breakfast to look at the Locks, five together, of which three are finished, the fourth about half-built, the fifth not quite excavated. Such an extent of masonry, upon such a scale, I have never beheld, each of these locks being 180 feet in length. It was a most impressive and remarkable scene. Men, horses and machines at work; digging, walling and puddling going on, men wheeling barrows, horses drawing stones along the railways. The great steam engine was at rest, having done its work. It threw out 160 hogs heads per minute [approximately 10,000 gallons] and two smaller engines (large ones they would have been considered anywhere else) were also needed while the excavation of the lower docks was going on: for they dug 24 feet below the surface of water in the river, and the water filtered thro' open gravel. The dredging machine was in action, revolving round and round, and bringing up at every turn matter which had never before been brought up to the air and light. Its chimney poured forth volumes of black smoke, which there was no annoyance in beholding, because there was room enough for it in this wide, clear atmosphere.'

Southey's descriptions hint at the mechanisation that had arrived in canal construction in the early nineteenth century. Steam engines kept the sites free of water and steam dredgers deepened the lochs. At Fort Augustus the canal entered Loch Ness, and from the far end of the loch it was only a short way to Inverness and beyond that to the coast at Clachnaharry. Unfortunately, however, the shoreline at this point has a gentle slope, so that deep water is only reached some distance from the coast. It was necessary to build an embankment out into the sea. Clay was dug out of a nearby hill and brought to the site on a specially constructed iron railway. This material was built into a bank that stretched out to sea for 400yds. Stones were laid on top and it was then allowed to settle for six months. Once the bank had been consolidated, the sea lock was built at the end. At first the site was kept pumped dry using a bucket dredger operated by a team of horses, but as the pit was sunk ever deeper into the bank, a small steam engine was brought to the site.

The canal finally opened in November 1822 but, by this time, Telford had already been at work on another ship canal in Sweden.

The idea for a canal that would cut across Sweden from the North Sea to the Baltic had been around for a long time. There was an obvious route that would connect a string of lakes, much as the Caledonian had done. A start was made as early as the sixteenth century when Gustavus Vasa planned to link Stockholm to the Göta River. The Eskilstuna River was canalised with the construction of eleven timber locks, linking two of the lakes, Hjälmaren and Mälaren, and was completed in 1610. In 1617 Dutch engineers improved the navigation on the Göta River. Things were moving forward, but the first canal proved unsatisfactory. Further sections were completed over the years, but the biggest obstacle was always the section between Lake Vänern and the Göta. Water from the lake entered the river via an imposing waterfall at Trollhättan. Work continued on improving the Göta, but the falls proved a major obstacle, and for years goods had to be carried round by land. The problem persisted right up to 1790 when a new company was formed to solve the problem. The engineer was variously known as Erik Nordwall and Nordewall. His answer was to carve a way through the rocks to create two lock staircases, one of three locks and one of five, to raise the waterway up to the level of the lake. A short section of canal was then cut to reach the lake itself. This new canal was named after the town, the Trollhätte Canal.

The older navigation attempts had not been successful but a new personality drove developments forwards – Count Baltzar von Platen. He was a naval officer who had risen to the top of the Swedish navy and, on his retirement, took a keen interest in improving navigation. He had been one of the men behind the Trollhätte Canal and now he wanted to extend it across the country to complete the system that had been thought about but not finished for two centuries. The man he looked to was a Norwegian engineer, Samuel Bagge, but Bagge didn't feel up to the task. In 1808 von Platen discussed his plans with King Gustav IV who issued a royal decree requesting Thomas Telford to take on the task. von Platen translated the document into wayward English. It requested Telford 'to

The locks of the Trollhättan Canal that lift it from the level of the River Göta to Lake Vanern. The work began in 1790 under the direction of the engineer Erik Nordewall. He carved his way through solid rock to create two lock staircases: one of three locks and one of five locks. In time these proved inadequate and were replaced by a single staircase, built alongside the original. Finally, in the twentieth century they too were replaced by one giant lock, 9m deep. All three sets can still be seen at the site, although the original locks are now gateless and derelict. (*Anthony Burton*)

take a view of this undertaking and give his opinion and council thereupon'. Getting the communication to Telford proved problematical as the engineer was travelling from canal works to canal works. von Platen began a long correspondence with the engineer, which began in typically chatty fashion: 'You will I hope excuse me for introducing myself quite a stranger to You in this manner and I fear in Englisch is not the best sort.' Imperfect it may have been, but Telford's Swedish was non-existent. It is clear from the early exchange of letters that Bagge must have visited the works on the Caledonian and held Telford in high regard, which made their eventual working relationship that much easier.

It is remarkable that a canal was even being contemplated when Europe was still convulsed by the Napoleonic Wars. Other Scandinavian countries and Russia had signed a peace treaty with France but Sweden opted out, fearing the spread of revolutionary ideas. Russia decided that Sweden could be treated as an enemy state and seized Finland. Bagge was placed in a most awkward position. As a Norwegian, he too was officially a citizen of an enemy country, even if Norway and Sweden weren't at war. He had to leave the country. It also meant that the seas around Scandinavia were dangerous. Telford accepted the invitation to visit Sweden, but only if he could be assured a safe passage:

'But these Northern Seas are at present much infested with Danish and French privateers this makes a passage in a common trading Vessel to be attended with a risk from these armed Vessels – however trifling. I must therefore stipulate that I shall be taken up at Aberdeen and also landed at the same Place by either a Swedish or English ship of War.'

Telford ordered provisions for himself and his two companions for the journey, and the list is now framed and hung in the restaurant at the Institution of Civil Engineers. It included two dozen bottles of Madeira and the same of port; three dozen of cider; six dozen of porter; and half a dozen each of gin and brandy. This was balanced by copious quantities of tea, and there was also an order for 31½ pounds of lump sugar.

Telford duly arrived in Sweden and toured the likely route of the canal. Although, as with the Caledonian, the canal was only needed to link a series of navigable lakes, the problems were far greater. The canalised section ran for 53 miles, more than twice that of the Scottish canal, and the summit was higher at 85m (278ft). The descent from Lake Vattern would require fifteen locks, which Telford suggested should consist of four linked pairs and a seven-lock staircase. In view of the difficulties involved and the almost complete absence of workers skilled in canal construction in Sweden, the engineer felt that it was impractical to build on the scale he had used in the Highlands. The locks would be 32m by 7m (105ft by 23ft).

Telford completed his survey, establishing a real friendship with von Platen and returned to Scotland. There was now a major political upheaval. The King was held largely responsible for the debacle over Finland and was deposed in favour of a new ruler, the former commander-in-chief of Norway, who now became King Charles August. Positions were now reversed: Norway was a friend and Bagge could return to take charge of the workings, whereas Telford was now officially the citizen of an enemy country. In practice, this made no difference to Telford's position, and Bagge made his own situation clear:

> 'I don't wish to take orders from any man except you or the Baron [von Platen]. It was not for the sake of profit nor for the sake of commodity I did leave Norway, but you know the project has always laid at my heart … Neither trouble nor reflection should be spared in exercising your orders.'

Although Bagge was full of good intentions, he sadly lacked experience. His large workforce consisted of 900 soldiers, 200 labourers and 150 Russian captives who Bagge described as having 'defected on the road home being tired of their despotic government'. But they were no more experienced than the man in charge. Bagge constantly wrote to Telford, begging for advice and help. He asked for experienced workmen, especially those used to puddling as no one in Sweden knew the process apart from himself, and he had only a vague recollection. He also asked for masons and the necessary tools and equipment. Telford sent various items, including rails, wheelbarrows, picks and shovels for Bagge to copy, as well as detailed engineering drawings.

By 1812, the main workforce consisted of 5,000 soldiers spread out along the line. Things were going well when tragedy intervened: Bagge drowned in a boating accident. The British supervisors took over much of the work done by Bagge, but not without friction, particularly with one man, Simpson, who antagonised the workers by drinking with them, but without ever paying his way. This caused von Platen grief, but work went ahead. Major decisions needed to be taken.

Many of the canal fixtures, such as lock gates and movable bridges, were designed to be made from cast iron. Sweden had a long history as a provider of wrought iron of the finest quality, but there was no expertise in foundry work. They could all have been manufactured in Britain, but von Platen saw the opportunity to create a new industry for his country. With help sent from Hazeldine, the company that made so much ironwork for Telford, a foundry was established beside the canal at Motola, which became the centre of a large and important industrial complex. Work on the Göta Canal was not immune from the shortage of funds that plagued so many other canal schemes. von Platen bore the brunt of criticism when costs overran estimates, although given the size of the task and the inexperienced workforce, no one should have been too surprised. He sent a long letter to Telford in which he spoke bitterly of the charges against him, but ended on a positive note by pointing to two things: the critics could never get rid of his 'calmness and tranquility'

The Trollhättan Canal still carries commercial traffic. This ship has arrived from Göteborg and is negotiating the narrow final section of canal that runs from the top of the locks to Lake Vanern. (*Anthony Burton*)

nor could they stop 'so large an undertaking in so many ways connected with general welfare, after it was so far advanced'. He got the funds to finish the job.

The canal was finally completed in 1832 and to mark the occasion, the royal yacht *Esplandian* made the trip from coast to coast. Sadly, the men who had worked so hard to achieve this were not there to see it. Telford was 70 years old and not ready to make the long sea crossing; von Platen had died at the end of 1829. The canal proved an immense success, so much so that the original locks at Trollhättan had to be enlarged at various times to take ever larger vessels. Visitors to the site today can see the derelict remains of the original locks, their nineteenth-century replacements that are still in use by small craft and the single ship lock for larger vessels with a massive 9m drop. Paradoxically, it is the older Trollhätte Canal that still has a busy commercial carrying trade, with cargo ships passing through it to the industrial sites around Lake Vattern on a weekly basis.

The three ship canals suffered varying fates. The Gloucester and Sharpness thrived for a long time, and Gloucester developed into a major inland import, with docks surrounded by imposing warehouses. Those days are over, but Sharpness remains an active port; as a whole the waterway can be deemed a success. The Caledonian never lived up to its promise. The expected use by naval vessels never happened, mainly because the end of the Napoleonic Wars ended the threat to British shipping for many years. Its main use was by the fishing fleets, moving from coast to coast, and today its traffic consists almost entirely

The continuation of the route from Lake Vanern to the Baltic Sea was accomplished with the building of the Göta Canal under the direction of the chief engineer, Thomas Telford. The painting by Johan Christian Berger shows the grand opening of the canal on 26 September 1832. The royal yacht *Esplendian* is passing through the sea lock at Mem on an inlet of the Baltic. (*The Göta Canal Company*)

of pleasure craft. It did, however, succeed in one of its objectives – in providing much needed work for the hard-pressed Highlanders. The Göta Canal proved in many ways the most successful of the three, not only providing a much needed cross-country route but also acting as a powerful stimulus to new industries. All three did, however, have one thing in common: they extended the boundaries of canal construction both in terms of size and technology.

So far we have mostly looked at canals in Europe, but across the Atlantic a major canal network was also being developed.

Chapter 9

North America

Ideas for canal construction in North America were being put forward long before the US gained independence, leaving the British only in control in Canada. The first advocate for an artificial waterway was an unlikely candidate for the role – a Catholic Priest, Louis Joliet. He was born in Quebec in 1646 at the heart of French Canada and took holy orders, but his early enthusiasm died rapidly and, after just four years, he quit the priesthood to become a fur trader. This involved extensive travel and in 1673 he was appointed to find connections from the north down to the Mississippi. He and his companions found their way to the great river, joining it at what is now Memphis. It was a genuinely epic adventure and for much of the return journey they made their way back by water, joining first the Illinois River and then a tributary, the Des Plaines, before a short portage brought them to the Chicago River and on to Lake Michigan. Joliet's report pointed out that by digging a short canal, Lake Michigan could be joined to the Illinois to create a mighty continuous water system from Canada all the way to the Gulf of Mexico. The idea made a lot of sense and a canal was built on the line suggested by Joliet – but not until 1827.

The other idea mooted at much the same time was for a canal through the narrow neck of land joining the mainland to Cape Cod, that crooked finger of land pointing out into the Atlantic between Boston and New York. Samuel Sewell, a merchant from Sandwich, recorded in his diary for 26 October 1676 that a neighbour had shown him where the canal should be built. Again, nothing happened simply because the costs were prohibitive. At this time in the late seventeenth century, the population of the region was too small to support such an ambitious scheme. This scheme was finally put into practice in 1914. Canal construction was put to one side for another hundred years, and only really got under way after America had won its independence: by 1790 the young United States saw thirty canal companies being formed in eight of the original thirteen states. They were partly financed by the government, which over the years invested almost $400 million, but even that was dwarfed by the thousand million dollars put up by private investors.

The development of North America transport is inextricably tied to the continent's great rivers, such as the Mississippi, Missouri and, north of the newly defined border, the St. Lawrence. The idea of linking the rapidly developing major towns to the rivers by means of artificial canals was attractive, but there was a problem: few, if any, Americans had experience of canal construction. The problems are exemplified in the first major canal project in the fledgling US – the Middlesex Canal.

The canal was to link Boston to the Merrimack River at Chelmsford and the canal company received its charter in 1793. The principal promoter was Judge James Sullivan, the son of Irish immigrants, later to become governor of Massachusetts, and the job of superintendent went to Loammi Baldwin, who had been a colonel in the War of Independence. Baldwin had great energy but no knowledge of canal construction. He took himself off to Harvard University to study all the available books on English canals: he was about to undertake the construction of a major canal without having ever seen a lock except as an illustration in a book. He was in desperate need of a competent surveyor, but the only man he could find was a self-taught surveyor from his hometown of Woburn, Samuel Thompson. Thompson had little surveying equipment, but he and Baldwin set out to survey a likely route. Baldwin recorded in his diary that they met 'insurmountable obstacles'. These did not deter the party, but more worryingly the levels that Thompson took were hopelessly inaccurate. He recorded the rise from Boston as 68½ft, where it was actually 100ft, and the rise from the Merrimack as 25ft instead of 41½ft. Fortunately, Baldwin did not trust the results and turned to the only man he knew with experience of canal work, an English engineer called William Weston. The route was surveyed again and the errors corrected.

The 1822 painting by Jabez Ward Barton from the Billerica Historical Society Collection shows the Middlesex Canal at the point where it crossed the Concord River. A lock can be seen in the distance, by the horse. The more distant horseman, next to the boat, is trotting across the floating towpath that allowed boats to be towed by horses across the river to rejoin the artificial canal. The section on which the horseman is shown is actually a drawbridge that could be lifted to allow river traffic through. (*Billerica Historical Society*)

Work now went ahead on laying out the line of the canal and working out the required structures. There were to be two sources of water. The first was the Concord River that was to be crossed on the level, which presented an interesting problem. Traffic on the canal would be moved in the conventional way – barges pulled by horses – but how would they cope with the river crossing? The ingenious answer was to build promontories and the space in between was filled with a floating towpath. At the summit, water was supplied by Horn Pond. The company bought the existing grain mill and a small industrial complex grew up at the site that is now home to a canal museum. The twenty locks were built to generous proportions, 80ft long and up to 12ft wide. Most were built of stone, made watertight by hydraulic cement derived from volcanic material imported from the West Indies. This was effective but expensive, so some were constructed from wood. The canal was 27½ miles long and at one time there were 500 men at work. The ordinary labourers were paid $8 a month, roughly $110 at today's prices – unlike the British navvies who expected higher rates than usual for this specialised work, their American counterparts were paid the standard rate for the period. Skilled workers, such as stonemasons and carpenters, were paid $15 a month. The pay seems very low, but the company gave the men shelter and provisions. It was necessarily seasonal, with everything stopping in the

The photograph shows the falls on the Merrimack River. On the far side one can see the entrance to the Pawtucket Canal beside the long single-storey building, the gatehouse. This controlled the flow of water from the river into the canal system. When Francis Cabot Lowell came here in the early nineteenth century the canal system played an important role in bringing water to turn the wheels of his new textile mill in what was to become the city of Lowell, Massachusetts.

freezing winters. The canal was completed at the end of 1803 and was a great success. Traffic on the canal was mainly in flats hauled by mules, occasionally hoisting a simple sail, and a regular passenger service was introduced from the start.

The Middlesex Canal was not the only scheme considered for joining the Merrimack to the coast. The Proprietors of Locks and Canals on the Merrimack River also planned a canal to Newbury Port, but the Middlesex beat them to it and the earlier plan was dropped. But the men behind the other scheme had not given up. They developed the Pawtucket Canal, built to bypass the mile of falls and rapids near Chelmsford that dropped the river by 35ft. It proved far more valuable than they could have imagined. The textile industry of America was still in its infancy at the end of the eighteenth century, and although powered machines were taking over all the old processes carried out by hand by workers in their own cottages, the British tried their best to keep the details secret. Inevitably they leaked out, and one man who visited textile mills in England carried away in his head the details of the new power looms. His name was Francis Cabot Lowell and in 1814 he arranged for the first power loom to be built in America. Satisfied that it worked, he planned an

This illustration gives a closer view of the gatehouse seen in the previous photograph. Inside the gatehouse are a series of heavy sluice gates that are raised or lowered, using a water turbine for power. To the right of the building is the barge lock. The canals of Lowell are unusual in being both transport routes and power sources, although today they are only used by tourists. (*Miss E. M. Waine*)

industrial complex with a mill that would combine spinning and weaving. It was a small beginning but from it the great textile town developed that would bear his name, Lowell. The existing canal system was essential for its success and Lowell developed a new canal to bring the water from above the falls to power the mills of the new town. Unlike much of the American canal system, the canals of Lowell still survive.

It is an interesting and instructive story. In Europe, canals had mainly been built to serve existing industrial complexes. Here, the Middlesex Canal was mainly intended to bring primary produce such as timber to the developing towns and cities of Massachusetts. But once the canals existed, they served as a catalyst for industrial development.

Many of the earliest developments, although given the name of canal, were little more than river improvements, short stretches of artificial waterway built as lateral cuts to overcome difficult sections of the river. The Connecticut River was typical of such schemes. The river was an important trade route, but navigating it was difficult and arduous. The craft in use in the eighteenth century were mainly flats, poled up the river or drifting down with the current, and there were portages round the most difficult sections. The first major improvement was the construction of the South Hadley Falls Canal. Work began in 1793 and although it was just 2 miles long, it was a major engineering feat, involving carving a cutting 40ft deep and 300ft long through solid rock. Instead of locks, the difference in levels was overcome by an inclined plane. This was 230ft long with a vertical drop of 53ft. Instead of a railed track, as on the British planes, there was a stone ramp, covered by heavy planks. The caisson consisted of a wooden box, with folding gates at both ends. This would be lowered into the canal, the boat would float in, the gates would be closed and then the water would be drained out through sluices. Two water wheels, fed by canal water, raised or lowered the caisson, which was mounted on three sets of wheels of different sizes to keep it level when on the slope. This was a larger version of the devices used on the barrow runs on the Caledonian Canal, described on p117.

Although boatmen welcomed the canal, it was bitterly opposed by other interests, a scenario all too familiar to Europeans attempting river improvements. Fishermen complained that the dam, built to divert water to the canal, stopped salmon going upstream and mill owners claimed their water supply was affected. The canal company compromised and lowered the dam, but nature had the last word: the rebuilt dam was washed away in a flood. It was replaced, but went the way of the second. The canal company abandoned the struggle.

The next obstacle was the Bellows Fall in Vermont. Once again this was a short canal but with a lot of engineering packed into it. The falls had a drop of 50ft, so the mile-long canal actually had nine locks. As the nineteenth century dawned, work began on another heavily locked canal round the Montague Falls, with eight locks in 3 miles. The last and longest of the canals was the 6 mile Windsor Locks Canal, opened in the 1820s. At the end of the navigation a new town grew up. It was here that the river men, the timber-raft men and the powder men, transporting barrels of gunpowder, met and often quarrelled that ended in brawls. It was not a tranquil spot in its early days – a sprawling township of bars and brothels – but it gradually developed respectability. The canal may have disturbed the peace of this part of the country, but it made the investors happy, regularly returning handsome dividends. The canal is still in use, but now only by pleasure craft. Over a quarter of a century of construction, the Connecticut River had been tamed.

River improvement by building short stretches of canal spread across the country's inhabited regions in the east. One such scheme developed over the years from this system to what would become one of America's most imposing canals – the Chesapeake and Ohio. It began with the work of America's most famous hero, George Washington. The Potomac River was largely unnavigable in the early eighteenth century, with two major obstacles in the form of the Great and Little Falls, some 14 miles upstream from what is now Washington DC. George Washington introduced a Bill to the Virginia burgesses in 1774, calling for improvements to the river, but it was rejected because most of the delegates didn't see their constituents benefiting. Washington had another try, this time adding improvements to the James River, but before anything could be done, the war against British rule began and Washington had other matters to attend to. With peace and independence in 1783, Washington again campaigned for improved transport in the infant United States and, in particular, with connections with what was then referred to as the Ohio country. In 1784 he set out his ideas in a letter: 'Extend the inland navigation of the eastern waters; communicate them as near as possible with those that run westward; open these to the Ohio; open such as extend from the Ohio towards Lake Erie.' It was ambitious, but an essential part of the steady development of new territories being opened for settlement as emigrants moved ever further west.

Washington received enthusiastic support from the Governor of Virginia, Benjamin Harrison. He persuaded Washington to explore up to the headwaters of the Potomac, then known as the Patowmack, in the Appalachians and beyond to investigate the river systems on the far side. He set off in September 1784 with just one servant as company and, together on foot and horseback, they journeyed about 650 miles, during which they travelled along the Shenandoah and from there crossed to the Allegheny, eventually reaching the junction with the Ohio River. He reported back to Harrison and the result was the formation of the Patowmack Company, authorised to improve the river with a series of short canals, built to bypass the worst obstacles. If the scheme proved successful and the shareholders received a satisfactory return on their investment, which was considerable as shares were $400 each, then canal construction would be extended to other regions.

In 1784 Washington stayed at an inn at Bath, now Berkeley Springs, West Virginia. The owner, James Rumsey, who was also a builder and inventor, showed Washington a model of a boat he had devised to travel on the Potomac. It had a bow-mounted paddle wheel that operated poles that would lever the boat along against the current. Washington was impressed and when work started on improving the Potomac at Harper's Ferry he put Rumsey in charge of clearing rocks. As the canal scheme advanced the lack of engineers with experience in canal construction in the country became a real problem. Rumsey was made chief engineer. He had realised his original model was impractical and devised ways to work it by steam instead of by water power. We shall return to Rumsey's experiments later, but in the meantime, he was occupied with building a canal, for which he had no experience whatsoever.

Rumsey not only had the problem of blasting a passage through rocks beside the Great Falls and building locks to overcome the change in level but also coping with an inexperienced workforce. The men were a strange mixture of slaves, indentured workers and Irish immigrants. They received a daily rum ration, which the Irish found ways of supplementing as no doubt many were used to making illegal poteen. There were many drunken brawls. The indentured labourers were always trying to escape, and those caught were marked as troublemakers by having their heads shaved. Nevertheless, the work went ahead. Rumsey built a total of five lateral canals, the longest of which was three quarters of a mile long beside the Little Falls, but the most imposing was the Great Falls bypass with a flight of five locks and a deep cutting through a rock gorge. It had taken a lot of time, the money was all spent and attempts either to sell new shares or to get government finance both failed. The Pawtucket Company was wound up and a new company with an even wider brief was formed in 1824 – the Chesapeake and Ohio Canal Company.

Originally the canal was planned in three sections: the eastern from Georgetown on the Potomac to Cumberland; the middle crossing the Continental Divide; and the western that would end at Pittsburgh. Engineers estimated the total cost at more than $22 million, which investors thought was ludicrously high. The eastern section looked reasonable because, although it would be a long canal of 186 miles, it only needed seventy-four locks. The greatest difficulties were in the middle section, where the total ascent and descent totalled 1,961ft and involved building 246 locks in just 70 miles. The western section was less problematical, with 78 locks in 85 miles, but without the problematic middle section it had no value. It was decided to start on the eastern section to see how things went, and a new estimate came in at more than $5 million for the eastern part, which seemed much more manageable. It proved, like so many other canal contracts around the world, very optimistic.

Work began on the canal that was to link the Potomac to the Ohio, with suitable celebrations and euphoria, on an obvious date for patriotic Americans – 4 July 1828. The enthusiasm was misplaced: it took the next twenty-two years to complete. The company constantly ran out of money and got deeply into debt, largely because of the exorbitant prices land owners along the route demanded to allow the canal across their holdings. There was also no shortage of engineering problems. Much had been made in the original reports of the need for lock construction, but not much emphasis was placed on building

The unusual aqueduct bridge across the Potomac. It had originally been planned to end the Chesapeake and Ohio canal at Georgetown, but Alexandria, across the river in Virginia, had contributed greatly to the funds and they demanded a connection to the canal. The result was this unusual structure that served both as a roadway and canal aqueduct. Sadly this interesting structure has not survived. (*Library of Congress*)

eleven aqueducts along the route. They were mostly conventional structures, the longest (the Monocacy) being 516ft long. The Seneca aqueduct, however, was unusual in that it was also a lock. Apart from the aqueducts there was also the 3,118ft long Paw Paw tunnel. But the greatest challenge was not on the canal itself.

Alexandria, on the western bank of the Potomac, had contributed $250,000, hoping to make a direct connection to the proposed canal. This would have involved an aqueduct across the river, which was deemed too expensive. By 1830, however, attitudes had changed and the Alexandria aqueduct was authorised. It was remarkable. It had eight spans supported by massive stone piers set on the bedrock, with their tops 30ft above the high water mark. During the spring thaws, massive ice floes would sweep down the river, so to protect the piers granite ice breakers, like the more familiar cutwaters on bridges, were built out from the piers. Unlike conventional aqueducts, the superstructure was built out of stout timbers, with a wooden trough and a narrow carriageway alongside it. This is why the Alexandria is usually referred to as an aqueduct bridge. Built to serve the southern state of Virginia, it was used against the south in the Civil War, when the trough was drained and used as a bridge for Union troops.

The canal finally reached Cumberland in 1850 and in spite of the delays and financial problems, it was an undoubted success, with income from tolls reaching a million dollars in bumper years. It was never, however, extended westwards: by 1850 the world of transport was changing.

Among the many small canals built during the first great period of canal construction, one major undertaking stood out both because of its size and its importance in opening up the country. The Erie Canal, originally known as the New York Canal, was designed to join Albany on the Hudson River to Lake Erie. From Albany, barges could continue on the Hudson to New York. Like the Chesapeake and Ohio, there was a long time during which schemes were put forward without anything happening. This is hardly surprising. It was hugely ambitious and being promoted in a comparatively thinly populated country with little expertise in civil engineering. The idea was proposed in the New York State Legislature in 1808, which led to the formation of the New York Canal Commissioners (NYCC). They hoped to get funds from the United States Congress, but were unsuccessful. They still went ahead with surveys, athough there was an interruption to the work when war broke out with Britain, which of course included the British colony of Canada, and the US, and only resumed in 1814 when the peace treaty was signed.

The Erie Canal at Lockport, looking down the double sets of five-lock staircases. These were cut through solid rock and carried the canal down the Niagara escarpment. (*New York Public Librarie*)

The reports of the NYCC indicate the difficulties encountered by the surveyors in what was to a large extent virgin territory:

'In exploring the route of the canal, in a country but partially cleared, it was impossible for the engineer, in first running over it, to determine in many places, where the canal line would pass. After advancing some distance in a doubtful course, difficulties would be met which made it expedient to go back upon the line to some point, whence a more eligible course might be pursued.'

The engineers had many concerns, not least water supply. A later report pointed out that if they relied on rivers, the canal was liable to be inundated with the floods that followed the thaws in spring and would suffer from shortages in the autumn. Because of the severe weather conditions, large parts of the canal bank would have to be faced with stone to protect against gales and floods. All this added to the expense that, in the absence of support either from the government or neighbouring states, would all be met by the State of New York. In spite of all the difficulties, a route was laid out and construction finally got under way in 1817.

This was a massive project in every sense, running for 363 miles with a total rise from Albany to Lake Erie of 568ft. Engineering works included eighty-three locks and three major aqueducts. The Genesee River crossing was the most elegant, 802ft long and carried across swirling falls on nine semi-circular arches. The longest was the Cohoes at 1,188ft and the third was the more modest 744ft long Little Falls aqueduct. All three would have been considered important undertakings on any canal under construction at that time. It was decided to make the locks to generous dimensions, 90ft by 15ft, and there were two parallel sets of five-lock staircases built at Lockport. The NYCC argued that as the main cost was piling, it would not make much difference to the overall expense to make them large enough to take barges capable of carrying 30 tonnes. They did, however, indulge in cost cutting. Hydraulic cement depended on using imported material, so ordinary mortar was used, and the lock floors were made of timber: expedients that worked in the short term, but wouldn't last. They didn't need to last very long anyway as the planners had seriously underestimated how successful their canal would be. The locks had to be increased in size several times over the years and the channel widened and deepened until eventually it would take vessels carrying 240 tonnes.

The work was handed out to a large number of small contractors, and early on at least a large part of the workforce was made up of Irish immigrants, known by the disparaging name of 'bogtrotters'. In some ways it was appropriate, for part of the route ran through the swamps and marshes west of Syracuse. They were paid a miserable $8 a month, and slept in crude wooden shacks – and the 'monthly payment' did not mean that for every month they were on site they got paid. A month to the contractors consisted of twenty-eight days when they worked – stoppages for bad weather did not count.

The conditions in summer, particularly in the marshes, were atrocious. Sickness, generally referred to as 'swamp fever', was endemic. It was, almost certainly, in fact malaria. Official reports put disease down to 'the vegetable putrefaction which unavoidably takes place with the overflowing of those lands'. The annual report for 1820 described work as being held up by disease among the men:

> 'The excessive and long continued heat of the last season, subjected them to extensive and distressing sickness. Between the middle of July and the first of October, about one thousand men, employed on the canal, from Salina to Seneca river, were disabled from labor by this cause. Most of these men recovered.'

The report does not record how many failed to recover, and whether this implied that they were too sick to continue working or simply died of their illness.

Later, as work on the canal progressed, more and more men joined the workforce, many of them coming from established farms. One lesson they had learned in establishing homes

Unlike British canals, American canals obtained a considerable part of their revenue from carrying passengers in specially designed packet boats. This painting of 1837 by George Harvey shows a packet boat on the Erie Canal at Pittsford. One can see that this was intended to be a speedy service by the three horses moving at pace, controlled by a postillion. (*Memorial Art Gallery of Rochester*)

in the wilderness was how to clear the land. They invented a device for pulling up tree stumps: with a team of horses and half a dozen men they could clear forty stumps a day. They also developed a quick method of felling trees, by attaching a cable to the top and winding it in with a screw. They cleared brush, by using a plough with an additional horizontal cutter. The work now moved on at a better pace. Even so it was not until 1825 that the canal officially opened. The news was relayed from end to end of the waterway in a unique fashion. Cannons had been placed at intervals of eight to 10 miles: as the first boats reached the Erie, a cannon was fired. The noise was picked up by the next down the line and so on, until the news reached Albany, when the last shot was fired.

The canal may have cost millions to build, but it soon showed that it was good value for money. In 1825 it brought in revenue of $495,000, more than enough to cover interest on the debt. More than 13,000 vessels of various kinds used the canal in that year and, unlike its British counterparts, there was immense passenger traffic – 40,000 passed through Utica. Its success brought an upsurge in construction in other parts of the country.

The most important venture to follow the success of the Erie was the Wabash and Erie Canal, the longest ever built in North America. It ran for more than 460 miles from Toledo on Lake Erie to the Ohio River, and when completed was part of a waterway that reached from the Canadian border to the Gulf of Mexico. The key word there is 'when', for although work started in 1832, it was not completed throughout until 1853, by which time it was obsolete. There were many reasons for the delay. In the early days, work was handicapped by corrupt men in charge, specifically the chairman of the enterprise, Milton Strapp, and the secretary, Dr O. Coe, who between them embezzled more than $2 million of the company's funds. Another problem was, as on the Erie, terrible outbreaks of diseases among the 1,000-strong workforce. Cholera took a heavy toll and, according to legend, on one 40-mile stretch, a worker died for every two yards the canal advanced. As that would have wiped out the entire workforce several times over, it must be an exaggeration. But the death toll was undoubtedly high.

In the rush of canal construction following the Erie success, waterways spread over a great area of the country, the majority of the money coming from the public purse. Before work began, the NYCC had hoped to employ a British engineer to make up for the lack of local expertise. That never happened, and American canals developed in different ways from those of Britain. One notable difference was how many rivers were crossed on the level, usually by building a dam on the river to ensure a suitable depth for the actual crossing. And, as mentioned earlier, there was a very busy passenger trade, although comfort was not a prime consideration. Peter Stevenson, in his *Sketch of the Civil Engineering in North America* (1859), gave this account of life on a packet boat:

'About eight o'clock in the evening every one is turned out of the cabin by the captain and his crew, who are occupied for some time in suspending from the ceiling two rows of cots or hammocks, arranged in three tiers, one above another. At nine, the whole company is ordered below, when the captain calls the names of the passengers from the way-bill, and at the same time assigns to each his bed, which must immediately be taken possession of by its rightful owner on pain of his being obliged to occupy a place on the floor, would the number of passengers exceed the number of beds … I have spent several successive nights in this way, in a cabin only 40ft long by 11ft broad, with no fewer than 40 passengers; while the deafening chorus produced by the croaking of the numberless bullfrogs …was so great, as to render it often difficult to make one's-self heard in conversation, and, of course, nearly impossible to sleep. The distribution of the beds seems to be generally regulated by the size of the passengers; those that are heaviest being placed in the berths next to the floor …at five o'clock in the morning, all hands are turned out in the same abrupt and discourteous style, and forced to remain on deck while the hammocks are removed and breakfast is in preparation. This interval is occupied in the duties of the toilette… A tin vessel is placed at the stern of the boat, in which everyone washes and fills for his own use from the water of the canal, with a gigantic spoon formed of the same metal; a towel, brush, and a comb, intended for the general service, hang at the cabin door.'

Charles Dickens was another who travelled by canal in America, describing his experiences in his *American Notes* of 1842. The sleeping arrangements were similar to those described by Stevenson, but Dickens inevitably gave a more whimsical description: 'I found suspended on either side of the cabin, three long tiers of hanging book-shelves, designed apparently for volumes of the small octavo size… I began dimly to comprehend that the passengers were the library.' Yet in spite of this and other discomforts, 'there was much in this mode of travelling that I heartily enjoyed.' He even claimed to find it invigorating to run up on deck at five in the morning, 'scooping up the icy water, plunging one's head into it, and drawing it out, all fresh and glowing with the cold'. But it was the travel itself, being towed along by mules, that he enjoyed most:

'The fast, brisk walk upon the towing-path, between "that time and breakfast", when every vein and artery seems to tingle with health: the exquisite beauty of the opening day, when light came gleaming off from everything; the lazy motion of the boat, when one lay idly on the deck, looking through, rather than at, the deep blue sky; the gliding on at night, so noiselessly, past frowning hills, sullen with dark trees, and sometimes angry in one red, burning spot high up, where unseen men lay crouching round a fire; the shining out of the bright stars undisturbed by noise of wheels or steam, or any other sound than the limpid rippling of the water as the boat went on: all these are pure delights.'

Every canal enthusiast can identify with those words – even if most would rather get up later in the morning.

Canals were always seen as important in opening up the young US. The same could be said of Canada. Before the canal age, Canada had the rudiments of a continuous waterway system, stretching inland towards the middle of the continent, in the form of the St. Lawrence River and the Great Lakes. All that was needed was to link them together and to bypass any rapids and falls on the river. However, there were years of false starts before anything of great note was accomplished.

The first attempt to build a canal began in the days when the French controlled much of the country. The idea was to bypass the dangerous rapids north of Montreal, and because it was believed this would open up a route to China, the project was known as Canal de Lachine, the China Canal. The first plans were laid in 1689, but nothing came of them until they were revived in the 1820s by a Scots immigrant, John Redpath. It was never a complex construction problem, although it was built on a suitably grand scale to allow large vessels to use the waterway, with seven locks, each 30m by 6m, in the 14km canal. It was immediately effective in bringing trade to Montreal at the expense of Quebec, and was so successful that it had to be enlarged in the 1840s and again in the 1870s. Its commercial life ended in 1970, but it has reopened for pleasure boating.

The next attempt at canal building started in 1798 with a lock on the Sault Ste. Marie canal in Ontario, designed to give access to Lake Superior by avoiding the rapids on the St. Mary's River. All was going well until war broke out in 1812, and in 1814 American forces crossed the border and destroyed the lock. It was finally replaced in 1895, but on a different scale. The new lock was 274m by 18m, with the first gates to be operated electrically anywhere in the world.

Falls and rapids had been bypassed by portage throughout the early years of Canadian history, but there was no greater obstacle than that which faced anyone moving goods between Lake Ontario and Lake Erie: the Niagara Falls. The idea of a canal across the narrow strip of land between the two lakes only appeared indirectly. It had first been suggested in 1799 but nothing was done, but in 1816 a young man called William Hamilton Merritt appeared on the scene. He was actually born in Westchester County, New York in 1793, but his father had fought for the Loyalists in the War of Independence and, like many other Loyalists, moved north of the border after the war. Merritt bought an old saw mill on Twelve Mile Creek and later added a grain mill. He had problems with water supply, and conceived the idea of building a canal from the Welland River. He and some neighbours surveyed the route using a water level, basically the same instrument as that used by the Romans to build their aqueducts. They found a ridge in the way, which they calculated as 10m high; it is actually 20m. In 1818 Merrit put in a petition for the canal to the mill, but also added that it would now allow boats to pass the Niagara escarpment. Things moved forward, but as a result of the different surveys, a new line was proposed in

1824, this time descending to a point below the Falls at what became known as Merritton, now part of St. Catharine's. There were more alterations even after work started in 1824. The canal largely followed natural waterways, but at one section a major artificial canal had to be dug for 3km. It was known as the Deep Cut and earned the name as it was up to 20m deep in places. Stabilising such a deep excavation was problematical and on 9 November 1818 after a period of heavy rain, when work was almost completed, the cutting collapsed, burying several workers. The original plan of using the Welland as a feeder was abandoned, and a new channel was cut to the Grand River. The canal opened in 1829, with access to Lake Erie down the feeder. This proved inadequate and in 1831 a new final section was completed. Like the Sault Ste. Marie, the Welland was developed over the years as ships got bigger. The current version is actually the fourth Welland Canal and was completed in the twentieth century.

The largest canal scheme of the period had little to do with commerce initially, but was a response to the war with America. Even after peace was agreed in 1814, it was clear to the British that if the Americans had advanced to the St. Lawrence, they could have cut off a vital transport link. The military needed to get supplies and men to the border quickly

First Eight Locks of the Rideau Canal, the North entrance from the Ottawa River

The Rideau Canal was Canada's first major canal, the building of which was controlled by officers from the Royal Engineers. One of these officers was Colonel Henry Francis Ainslie who, as he travelled round the workings, kept a sketch book, with watercolour illustrations. This and the next two illustrations are from that book. This one shows the start of the canal at the Ottawa River, where it rises steeply through a flight of eight locks. It looks a lonely spot, but today it has been engulfed by the modern city and the Parliament Buildings stand next to the waterway. (*Archives of Ontario*)

and efficiently, and the best way would be via a canal linking the St. Lawrence to the Great Lakes. The Commission set up to investigate the idea added, almost as an afterthought, that it would benefit agriculture and commerce. They saw a great trade developing in timber being brought to Montreal, and suggested, optimistically, 'the result of this work, uniting the great waters of the St. Lawrence and the Ottawa, and offering a safe internal navigation, will turn a large portion of the present trade of New York towards Canada.' The plan was approved for what would become known as the Rideau Canal, but nothing was actually done.

As relations with the US improved, enthusiasm for the canal waned, but was rekindled when the renowned Duke of Wellington declared it essential. Lieutenant Colonel John Bey of the Royal Engineers arrived from Britain to take charge. His vision turned the original plans for a modest barge canal into something grander, with locks 133ft by 36ft. The survey was carried out by the military under Bey. It was to run from the mouth of the Rideau River, at what is now Ottawa, through a series of small lakes to the Cataraqui River that joined Lake Ontario at Kingston. The 204km route was a mixture of natural waterways with artificial canal and included the construction of forty-seven locks as well as dams and weirs on the river sections.

Although the work was supervised by officers of the Royal Engineers overseen by Bey, the actual construction was let out to small contractors. However, two companies of the Royal Sappers and Marines, each consisting of eighty-one men, were brought from

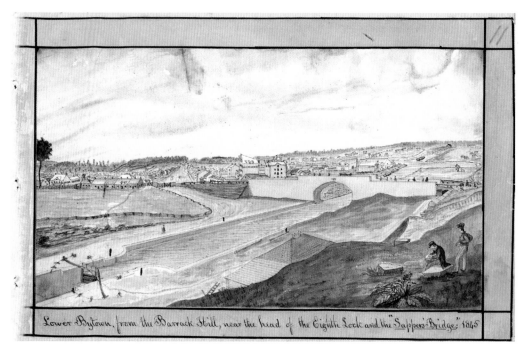

Lower Bytown, from the Barrack Hill, near the head of the Eighth Lock and the "Sappers' Bridge." 1845

This view, looking down from Barrack Hill, shows a lock and a bridge that is a reminder of the military role in building the canal – Sappers' Bridge. (*Archives of Ontario*)

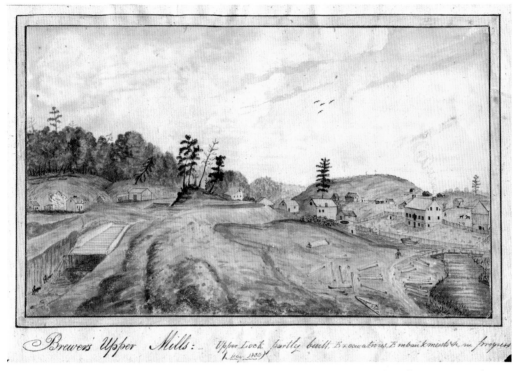

Brewer's Upper Mills :_ Upper Lock partly built, Excavations, Embankments &c in progress

This is one of the few early sketches by Ainslie that shows construction actually still in progress. The site was described as Brewer's Upper Mills and a half completed lock. A figure can just be made out with a wheelbarrow at the bottom of the lock chamber. (*Archives of Ontario*)

England and their work included both guard duty and, when necessary, construction work. Many of the men stayed on after the work was completed and settled along the line of the canal. It was never going to be easy, building through what was, in effect, mainly an uninhabited wilderness; many of the contractors finished up bankrupt. The workforce was made up of local French Canadians and large numbers of Irish immigrants. The conditions were much like those on the Erie Canal, and the results were just as dire. Many men died of 'swamp fever'. Bey decided that work should go on through the winter, when the workers would not be struck down by malaria. He also pointed out that although breaking through frozen ground would be difficult, the supplies could be brought in more cheaply: it is easier loading stuff onto sledges than putting it on carts that had to travel across unsurfaced roads. Because of the transport difficulties as much as possible had to be carried out on the spot: quarries were opened to provide the stone for locks, trees felled for housing and blacksmiths made the ironwork. Work went well and the canal opened by 1832. Nearly two decades after peace had been declared, the canal still had a military air: lock houses were fortified and blockhouses were erected for troops who would never need to use them.

One of the greatest problems was the lack of experienced workmen. In his story of the canal, *Rideau Waterway* (1972), Robert Legget quotes John MacTaggart, who had come over from Britain to take on the job of Clerk of Works, He described what happened when Irish immigrants were brought to the workings:

'Even in their spade and pickaxe business, the [men] receive dreadful accidents; as excavating in a *wilderness* is quite a different thing from doing that kind of thing in a cleared country. Thus they have to *pool in* as the tactics of the art go – that is, to dig beneath the rots of trees, which not infrequently fall down and smother them.'

Some men left, tempted by better wages, for the stone quarries, work with which they were totally unfamiliar. The results were inevitable:

'Of course, many of them were blasted to pieces by their own *shots*, others killed by stones falling on them. I have seen heads, arms, and legs, blown in all directions, and it is vain for overseers to warn them of their danger, for they will pay no attention.'

The Rideau Canal in modern Ottawa. In summer it is used by pleasure boats, and in winter it becomes a popular elongated skating rink. (*Tony Webster*)

The Rideau Canal was initially successful as it offered a far better transport system to the Great Lakes than travelling down the St. Lawrence, which was still largely unimproved and famous for its hazardous rapids. But in the 1840s, work started on improving the St. Lawrence and the glory days of the Rideau ended. It might have gone the way of so many other canals in North America, but the country through which it passed still had few decent roads. It remained in business long enough to be appreciated as a tourist attraction and is now a popular route for holiday boaters.

Rivers had always been vital in opening up North America to European settlers, and canals were just as important in linking the various systems. They were vital for trade in goods and for moving people around the country. They also introduced innovations, some of which we will look at next.

Chapter 10

Connecting Links

Certain terrains would always make canal construction difficult, if not impossible. The inclined plane method of overcoming sudden changes in level has already been discussed. This came in various forms, from the simple tub–boat canals, which were often self-acting, with the heavier downward load raising the empty tubs on a parallel track, to the more sophisticated versions worked by steam engines. The most dramatic use of inclined planes was on the Morris Canal. The canal had its origins in a sound commercial idea – to link the industrial region round Pittsburgh with New York. The distance between Pittsburgh and Newark Bay was about 55 miles, but the direct route was impossible, and a more roundabout line had to be taken that meant the finished canal was 102 miles long. Even then there were formidable obstacles. To cross the hills around Lake Hopatcong involved a 914ft climb up one side and a 760ft drop on the other. The Morris Canal and Banking Company was formed with the idea of selling stock worth $2 million – in the

The photograph shows inclined plane Number 9, one of twenty-three similar inclines on the Morris Canal in America. Boats are lifted by means of a water turbine controlled from the tower that can be seen at the top of the slope. (*Canal Society of New Jersey*)

event work started in 1829 with just a million in the kitty and no clear plan how to cross the mountains.

The solution was proposed by Professor James Renwick of Columbia University. His plan was to use just twenty-three locks and twenty-three planes. The latter were very sophisticated. Each incline had a power house at the top. Beneath it was a reaction turbine, set into a well. When a boat needed to be moved the operator opened a valve, and water from the upper level rushed down the well to work the turbine. This connected with a drum, round which a cable was wound that was attached to a cradle on the plane. The boats themselves were flat-bottomed and easily floated on and off the cradle. It was recorded that a barge, loaded with 70 tonnes of coal, could be raised for a vertical distance of 100ft in just a quarter of an hour. Given that to cover this vertical distance would probably have required a dozen locks to be built, the expense of building the incline and power house looks like a sound investment. And using one incline instead of a string of locks was an immense saving in journey time. It was a triumph and by 1860 it was carrying more than 700,000 tonnes of coal and pig iron a year. Unlike most other American canals, however, it was never used for passengers. It remains one of the engineering triumphs of the American canal age.

An alternative to the inclined plane was a vertical lift. One early attempt at getting up a steep rise without an incline was on the Somerset Coal Canal. The canal was built to bring coal from the mines at Poulton and Radstock to the Kennet & Avon at Dundas. The biggest problem was the steep hill at Combe Hay. The engineer Robert Weldon devised the ingenious caisson lock. Although nominally a lock, it was more like a large well. The caisson was a metal box, with watertight doors at either end. Boats could enter the caisson through a short tunnel, after which air was pumped into the box, which floated up to the top of the lock, guided by rails in the side of the well. The doors at the far end could then be opened and the boats could continue on their way. It was not a success and was soon replaced by an inclined plane, and that in turn was removed and a conventional flight of locks was built. The canal has long since been abandoned, but traces of the locks remain, with iron gates. The site of the unique lock is identified by being close to the building still known as Caisson House, but although excavations have revealed just where it was situated, no details have survived to give any clearer indication of exactly how it was built. One can only assume, as the entrance was through a tunnel, that the boatman had to steer his vessel into the caisson. Being shut into a floating box must have been like being enclosed in a miniature submarine.

A more satisfactory form of vertical lock was developed for the Grand Western canal. This venture began optimistically but staggered to a conclusion of sorts, rarely repaying the effort needed to finance and build it. The original scheme was for a canal that would link Exeter to Bristol, as part of a through route for 50 tonne barges all the way to London. The first bad decision was not to start at Exeter at all, but at Tiverton, simply because of the possibility of quick profits carrying stone from local quarries. The engineer was John Rennie and work got under way in 1809, a mere thirteen years after the first proposal. It was to be a contour canal, threading its way through a hilly landscape on a route that involved one colossal U-bend and a section cut into a hillside. Three years later, the canal had reached Holcombe Regis, just 11 miles from Tiverton but having already cost more than the amount estimated for the whole canal. Everything now stopped, and although the canal did have traffic in stone, the revenue never amounted to £1,000 in any one year; not much of a return for an investment of a quarter of a million pounds.

Nothing now happened until the opening of the Bridgwater & Taunton Canal in 1827. It offered the possibility of making a useful connection for the first time for the Grand Western, and the work of extending the latter to Exeter went to a local engineer, James Green. His plans were radical. There would be no conventional locks, just one inclined plane and a series of seven vertical lifts.

The incline plane would work on the hydraulic principle. The weight of the boat going up the plane would be counterbalanced by a large bucket of water falling in a shaft, the bucket being emptied for a boat going in the opposite direction. It was not a success, and a steam engine had to be installed to take over the work. The idea of vertical lifts was not

The Anderton lift was built to move boats between the River Weaver and the Trent & Mersey Canal at the higher level. Built in the nineteenth century it was originally powered by means of a hydraulic ram and two counterbalanced caissons, but was converted to electric power in 1902. The caissons are now separately counterbalanced so can be moved individually. (*Mike Peel*)

This photograph, probably taken in the 1950s, shows two working boats floating in one of the caissons on the Anderton lift. Each caisson is 75ft long and 15ft deep, designed either to take one barge off the Weaver Navigation or a pair of narrow boats from the Trent & Mersey. (*Anthony Burton*)

entirely new. But Green's were the first put into use on a working canal. They worked on a counterbalance system. Boats could be floated into one or other of a pair of caissons, linked by chains. When one caisson was at the top of the lift, the other would be at the bottom. By adding water to the upper caisson it fell, its descent controlled by a brake, while the other one rose. The system worked, and although the canal has long since closed, remains of these unique lifts can still be found.

The idea was not followed through with great enthusiasm by other engineers until 1875. Edward Leader Williams, the engineer in charge of improvements to the Weaver Navigation, designed a lift to link it to the Trent & Mersey Canal, 50ft above the river. The lift contained a pair of caissons, each 75ft long, 15ft wide and 5ft deep, weighing 250 tonnes and capable of taking the flats that were in use on the Weaver or the narrow boats of the canal. Set within a massive iron frame, they were originally designed to be counterbalanced and moved by hydraulic rams. The approach from the Trent & Mersey was via a short aqueduct that could be closed off with timber gates with watertight seals. Unfortunately the water used for the rams came from the polluted canal, which damaged the sealants. In 1902, the hydraulic system was replaced by electric motors, and the lift still in use today no longer relies on each caisson counterbalancing the other. Instead, a system of weights hung round the frame in seemingly haphazard fashion do the job, and each caisson moves independently. Lifts of this type, many on a much larger scale, were built and remain in use in North America, Canada and mainland Europe, culminating in the lift at Strépy-Thieu on the Canal du Centre, Belgium. Completed in 2002, it can raise 1,350 tonne barges to a height of 73m. It is still the mightiest lift of its kind, but is due to be overtaken by a new lift in China. The prize for the most unusual boat lift must, however, go to Scotland and the Falkirk Wheel, completed in 2002. Built to reunite the Forth & Clyde and Union Canals,

Starting in 1888, an imposing set of four lifts was built for the Canal du Centre in Belgium. Together with two locks they covered a rise of 70m. Although no longer in use, they have been preserved as historic monuments and have been given UNESCO World Heritage status. The photograph shows lift number 3. (*Tenger*)

The four lifts on the Canal du Centre were replaced in 2002 by this immense lift at Strépy-Thieu. Where the old lifts could only take barges up to 300 tonnes, the new version takes 1,350 tonne barges the full 70m in a single lift. The caissons are counterbalanced: one can be seen at the top of the lift at the right-hand side; the other is at the bottom on the left. (*Raymond Speleking*)

the balanced caissons follow a circular path round giant concrete hoops. When one caisson is aligned with an aqueduct that reaches the wheel at the Union Canal at the upper level, the other is at the level of the Forth & Clyde below.

But there were limits to what even the most ambitious lifts and planes could achieve. Throughout the canal age, waterways were by far the most efficient way of moving goods and if the terrain made it impossible for a canal to reach a particular industrial site then other ways had to be found to bring cargo to canal or river. The answer was to use railed tracks, known as tramways.

The earliest version was developed in Germany. The classic account of mining and metal working, *De Re Metallica* (1556) by Agricola, shows a mine in which carts run along a fixed wooden track. They are kept on the track by means of pins sticking out from the bottom of the trucks that run in a groove in the centre of the planks. The system became more sophisticated when parallel wooden rails were laid and trucks were given flanged wooden wheels. Tramways became part of the mining scene in many parts of Europe, with many variations. In some systems plain wheels ran inside the rails, but by the eighteenth century the advances in iron production saw a more hardwearing type of tramway come into use. Rails were made of cast iron, generally with an L-shaped cross section to hold the wheels in place. A large network developed in mining areas, especially the north east of England. As the collieries were higher up than the river, all the loads went downhill. The man in charge controlled the descent by means of a handbrake and the horse trotted along behind. Then the horse was harnessed to the cart for the return journey with the empty waggon.

Among the earliest tramways built in Britain were those connecting the collieries of Northumberland to the River Tyne. The illustration shows a typical wagonload of coal running downhill towards the river, controlled by the driver using the crude curved handbrake. The horse, trotting along behind, will be needed for the uphill return journey. It would appear that the rails are L-shaped, with vertical flanges inside the wheels. The tramway ends at Staithes like those seen on the opposite bank, where the coal is being dropped down a chute into a barge. (*Anthony Burton*)

A tramway, designed by Benjamin Outram, brought coal from Denby to the Derby Canal and survived in use long enough to be photographed. The wagon design has changed very little from that shown in the early drawing, but there is one significant change. The coal was actually carried in boxes, designed to fit snugly into the hold of the narrow boat – an early example of containerisation. (*Waterways Archive Gloucester*)

In Britain, the tramways became an integral part of some canal systems. A good example is the Brecon & Abergavenny Canal in South Wales. The name is misleading, as it never actually goes to Abergavenny; instead it begins with an end-on meeting with the Monmouthshire Canal at Pontymoile. The Monmouthshire Canal makes economic sense, serving an industrial area of mines and foundries and connecting them to coastal traffic at Newport. The Brecon & Abergavenny, however, sets off on a wandering track, high up a hillside on the edge of the Brecon Beacons, and scarcely touches town or village until it reaches the terminus at Brecon. But the surrounding hills were full of busy industries, from stone quarries to ironworks, and fourteen different tramways were built to create profitable traffic for the canal.

The remains of many of these tramways can still be traced from the canal, often revealed by the sleepers – tell-tale parallel rows of stone blocks with holes in the centre. We are used to seeing railways with sleepers stretching across and under both tracks, but the tramways were worked by horses, which would constantly have been tripping over them. So wooden plugs were inserted in the holes and the rails spiked to the stones, leaving a clear track in between. The most interesting tramway was built by the Hill family, who owned extensive ironworks at Blaenavon, some 4 miles from the canal in a direct line, but separated from

The Brecon & Abergavenny Canal was served by a complex system of tramways, some stretching many miles away from the canal. Thomas Hill established the Blaenavon ironworks (see p.00) in 1789 and built a tramway from the works to the canal with a branch running off to stone quarries. Although the tracks have long since gone, this section can still be clearly seen high up on the hill, Blorenge, as a flat track hugging the contours. (*Anthony Burton*)

it by steep hills. Much of the route can still be followed, and it shows just how important the connection was, as well as the engineering solutions, to make the whole system work.

The ironworks were established at Blaenavon in 1789 and work on the canal began four years later. The Hills immediately pressed the canal company to complete the works to Pontymoile so that they could send out their iron. By 1795 they began developing the tramway that would lead from the works to Llanfoist on the canal, with a continuation down to the main road further down the hill. Llanfoist is a spot full of interest. The tramway was carried over the canal on a flat-topped bridge, before continuing down what is now a roadway. Access to the extensive wharf area by road is via a tunnel under the canal. There are two notable buildings on the site. The first is a warehouse on two levels. At the upper level, grooves in the floor suggest the trucks were run straight in. Boats floated right into the lower level for loading. Next to it is Canal House, with little windows on the top floor, looking down both at the wharf and up the hillside at a track that marks the line of the tramway. Walking up the track reveals the typical stone blocks, and halfway up is a platform, above which the track continues on a different alignment. There would originally have been a winding drum here. These are the two inclines that between them took the line through a total vertical of 550ft. The line now emerges on a bracken-covered hillside, and follows the natural contours to a point known as The Tumble, where it goes through a dramatic U-bend. Here one branch leads off to limestone quarries, and the main line disappears into a tunnel, only to emerge again at the ironworks. These are remarkably well preserved, with imposing blast furnaces, and a big tower structure in the centre. This was the water-balance lift, working much like a vertical canal lift, to move trucks and material between the top and bottom of the site.

Travelling the Brecon & Abergavenny Canal today is a joy thanks to its rural quiet and magnificent scenery, and Llanfoist is as peaceful as anywhere. Only the tramway remains hint at what it must once have been like, with the different wharfs filled with stone and iron and the peace disturbed by the rattle of chains and the clatter of wheels as the trucks were hoisted up and down the inclines. The system did not always work perfectly. The

The building of a canal to link Philadelphia to Pittsburgh had to cope with the fact that the Alleghenies ran right across the line of the route. It was decided to use a series of inclined planes, but instead of linking them in the conventional way by intermediate canals, the boats would be moved along a special Portage Railway. The passenger boats were designed so that they could be divided into two halves, floated onto wheeled carriages and then either hauled up the slopes by cables or pulled on the level by horses. The illustration shows a sectioned boat ascending one of the planes. The Portage Railway was later the scene of one of America's first attempts to use steam locomotives. (*Anthony Burton*)

Duke of Rutland gave this account of a harrowing experience on one of the Brecon & Abergavenny tramways in his book, *Journal of a Tour through North and South Wales,* 1805:

'Last year, Mr. Frere, the proprietor of the ironworks, was returning from London, and going along the rail-road in a post-chaise, when about a hundred yards from him, he saw one of those wagons coming down upon him with astonishing velocity. He could not possibly get out of the way, and must have been crushed to pieces, if fortunately the waggon had not broken over the iron groove, which had hitherto kept it in the track, and run forcibly up an ash-tree by the side of the road, in the branches of which it literally stuck, and thus saved him from immediate destruction.'

The tramways were essential to many of the Welsh canals, but one man mistrusted them, as potential rivals. The Duke of Bridgewater remarked that canals would do well enough 'if they kept away from those damn'd tramroads'. He was an accurate prophet, as we shall see in the next chapter.

One American canal combined inclines and tramways in a unique way. The canal was designed to link the Susquehanna and Allegheny Rivers, in effect joining Pittsburgh to Philadelphia. Work got under way in 1826. Two experienced engineers were brought in, both of whom had worked on the Erie Canal: James Geddes and Nathan Roberts. Their surveys showed them that it would be impractical to cross the Alleghenies by water. Work had started at both ends, and the two engineers planned to bring the eastern section up to the foot of the hills that reared up to a height of more than 2,000ft. That left a gap of 26½ miles that would be closed by a mixture of railed track and inclines – the Portage Railway. What distinguished this system from other similar mixtures was the design of the packet boats. These looked conventional enough while working on the canal, but could be divided into two parts for movement along the Portage Railway. With its various branches, the canal ran for a total of 606 miles, not just the longest in America but, with a final cost of more than $10 million, by far the most expensive.

When the line between Philadelphia and Pittsburgh finally opened in 1834, the world was already moving into a new transport era that had its origins in events that began more than a century before.

Chapter 11

The Steam Age

The steam engine evolved as a response to a pressing problem. Mines, especially the tin and copper mines of the south west of England, needed to go ever deeper to reach the ore, but the available pumps couldn't cope with removing water from such depths. The first successful solution was provided by a Dartmouth man, Thomas Newcomen, who had supplied miners with tools and was aware of the problem, as described on p.69. The first Newcomen engine worked at a colliery at Dudley in the Midlands in 1712. Collieries were the main beneficiaries of the invention, and its inherent inefficiency was no problem where coal was so readily obtainable. But as its use spread to other areas, notably the metal mines of Devon and Cornwall, the situation was different. There coal, mainly brought in by sea from South Wales, was very expensive. Attempts were made to improve the engine, but very little changed for half a century. It was this machine, however, that led directly to a true steam engine.

James Watt was an instrument maker at Glasgow University when he was sent a model of a Newcomen engine that wasn't working. He realised there was an inherent inefficiency caused by constantly cooling and then reheating the cylinder. His solution was to condense the steam in a separate vessel so that the cylinder could be kept permanently hot. To solve the problem of heat escaping from the open top, he closed off the top of the cylinder and, instead of air pressure, used the pressure of steam to push down the piston. The atmospheric engine had become a far more efficient true steam engine.

Watt went into partnership with the Birmingham industrialist Mathew Boulton. They established a new works to manufacture steam engines on a site beside the Birmingham Canal. Boulton's other factory was the Soho works a few miles away, so this became the Soho Engine Works. This was still the meandering Birmingham Canal as laid out by James Brindley. Early in the nineteenth century, Telford made major improvements, slicing through the old wobbly route in a new straight line canal. There was no question of closing off the original canal, simply because there were so many businesses, including important customers, lining the banks. So the bends were left as loops off the main line, and the one containing the Boulton & Watt factory remains the Soho loop to this day.

The steam engine came into use on the canals as a pumping engine for water supply. There are old engine houses on many canals around the country, including one on the Birmingham Canal. A few still have their old engines in place, including one on the Cromford Canal, but

This Boulton & Watt engine of 1776 was built to supply water for the summit level of the Birmingham Canal. The photograph was taken as the building was being demolished. It is typical of early pumping engines, with the pump rods suspended from one end of the beam, and with the piston rising above the steam cylinder attached to the opposite end of the beam. James Watt's engines were massive and worked at very low pressures, and it is difficult to imagine such a cumbersome machine being adapted for any form of transport. (*Science and Society*)

there is only one place where a pumping engine can, and still does, work exactly as it did when first installed, and that is on the Kennet & Avon at Crofton. The water source is a lake below the level of the canal. The engine house itself contains two massive engines, one of which is a Boulton & Watt of 1812. It is remarkable to think that this magnificent machine started its working life when Napoleon was setting off on the long, dismal trudge with his defeated army back from Russia. The machines may look archaic, great lumbering, slowly nodding beam engines, but they are still powerful, able when working together to pump a million gallons an hour. It is one of those sights that inspires awe, as water gushes into the leat that carries it away to the canal summit. But for all their power, these are still engines working at low steam pressure, and can do so much work simply because of their size.

Watt had a virtual monopoly on all steam engine construction until the end of the eighteenth century thanks to an all-embracing patent. He did make one significant improvement.

Originally, as in the Newcomen engine, the piston was hung from the beam by a chain, which meant it still needed a weight at the other end of the beam: you can pull a chain but can't push it. Making a rigid connection was problematic as the end of the beam moves along a circular path. Watt solved this by attaching the top end of the piston rod to a shifting parallelogram of rods. Now steam pressure could move the piston in both directions – and that meant it could be used, via a crank, or some similar device, to turn a shaft. It could drive machinery. The steam age was about to enter a second, vital period of development. In the latter part of the eighteenth century, several ideas had been put forward for applying steam power to moving boats: some were practical, others less so. It might have been expected that the first success would have come in Britain, where steam power had been developed, but it is generally agreed that the first successful steamer appeared across the Channel in France.

The story of canals has largely been one of practical, working men, often with very little formal education, who learned by experience rather than theory. The next developer in the steam world definitely does not fit that mould – Claude-Françoise-Dorothée, Marquis de Jouffroy d'Abbans. Born in 1751, he entered the army at 20, was involved in a duel and then exiled from Paris. He took an interest in steam power, starting by studying pumps. He experimented with using steam to power a boat. His first experiment on the River Doubs in 1778 was not a success, largely because he tried to use the engine to work 'duck feet' paddles. He then embarked on a much more ambitious project, when in 1782 he designed the 182 tonne *Pyroscaphe* for which he developed a double-ratchet system, to turn continuously rotating paddle wheels on each side of the vessel. He applied for a patent, and produced a model of his vessel for inspection, now preserved in the Musée de la Marine in Paris. The vessel underwent trials on the Saône near Lyon in 1783. The French academicians prevaricated over the patent and before anything more could be done, the

A model presented to the French Académie de Science by the Marquis Jouffroy d'Abbans to persuade them to allow him to build a full-size paddle steamer and test it on the Seine in Paris. He was refused permission. In the event, his trials took place on the River Saône near Lyons, starting in 1775 and were eventually successfully completed with his vessel, the *Pyroscaphe*, launched in 1783. Unfortunately further developments in France were halted by the great political revolution. (*Musée de la Marine*)

country was convulsed by revolution. The Marquis abandoned his schemes, although he did write a treatise on steamships. It was a bold beginning, but it is uncertain how many people outside France were aware of the events.

An alternative to the paddle steamer was tried in America in the 1780s. A steam pump drew in water at the bows and fired it out at the stern, but the technology of the time was not up to it. The next successful experiment took place in Britain. William Symington was born at Leadhills in Scotland in 1764, a spot that as its name suggests was at the heart of a lead mining district, where his father worked as an engineer. The local school recommended that he should train for the clergy, but instead he followed his father's profession. He soon showed a strongly inventive mind and thought of ways to improve the Boulton & Watt engine at the local mine. He also tinkered with building a steam carriage to go on the road. In 1787, an Edinburgh banker, Patrick Miller, invited Symington to design the engine for a paddle steamer.

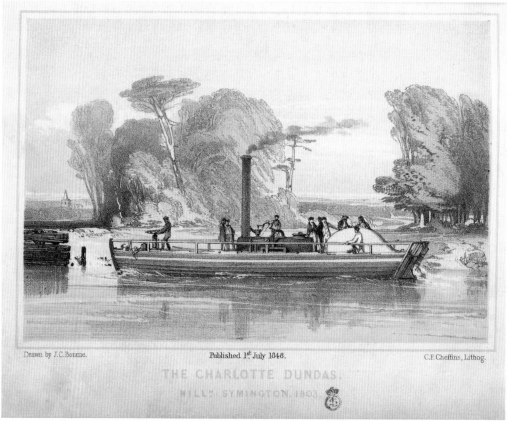

Drawn by J.C.Bourne.   Published 1st July 1848.   C.F.Cheffins, Lithog.

THE CHARLOTTE DUNDAS.
WILL™ SYMINGTON, 1803.

The steamer *Charlotte Dundas* was designed by William Symington as a tug to haul barges on the Forth & Clyde Canal. At its trials in 1802 it proved successful in hauling two 70 tonne barges at an average speed of slightly over 3mph. The authorities, however, were worried that the wash from the paddle wheels would damage the banks. The experiment was abandoned. (*Science and Society*)

The vessel was a double-hulled 25ft vessel with a small engine made in a local brass foundry. It was tried out on Dalswinton Loch in Dumfries in 1788, achieving a speed of 5mph. Among those invited to try out the novel system was the poet Robert Burns. Unfortunately he left no record of his adventure, but he could at least claim to be the first poet to be moved by steam. Encouraged by this success, Symington made arrangements for a much larger engine to be built at the famous Carron Ironworks. In 1789, there was a fresh trial on the Forth & Clyde Canal, but the paddle wheels broke. Miller was furious and blamed Symington, who he described as a vain fool. The steamboat experiment was abandoned, and Symington returned to more conventional engineering projects.

Symington, however, never abandoned his steam ideas and continued experimenting with different types of rotary engines. Then, in 1800, Lord Dundas, one of the directors of the Forth & Clyde Canal Company, asked him to build an engine for a boat designed by Captain John Shank, for use on the canal. The vessel was named *Charlotte Dundas* after the director's daughter. It proved underpowered, but a second version, *Charlotte Dundas II*, was soon completed. It was very simple, with steam provided by a rough waggon-boiler, with the flues encased in brick. The single 22 inch diameter cylinder was set horizontally, with the piston connected directly to a crank to drive the wheel. In tests on the canal in 1802, it towed two 70 tonne barges against a strong headwind for 20 miles at an average speed of about 3mph. In that respect, it was a success, but a new problem appeared. Boulton & Watt were always jealous of anyone else developing any form of steam power, and their engineer James Lawson reported, rather gleefully, on the outcome: 'The Engine is made by Symington & turns a Wheel – which made so much Splashing that they were affraid of washing down the Canal Banks … the papers say Lord Dundas is the great Patroniser of the scheme – which I rather think will Die without further noise.' Lawson was almost right. The canal company did indeed decide that the vessel was likely to cause too much damage to the canal banks and abandoned the scheme. The Duke of Bridgewater was impressed, and ordered eight similar craft for his canal. Sadly, he died before the order was completed, and his successors showed no further interest. The pioneering canal tug was left to rot and Symington's boat building days were ended. The scene moved across the Atlantic for the next stage of development.

Developing steamboats for American waterways had begun early. John Fitch was born in Windsor, Connecticut, in 1743 and had a varied career. He had little formal schooling and was apprenticed to a clock maker, then he tried to set up in business as a brass founder and, when that failed, began a brass and silversmith business. The American Revolution ended that and he worked as a gunsmith for the New Jersey militia during the war years. He also set up a profitable business supplying beer and rum to the troops. By 1780 he was acting as a land surveyor in Kentucky when he was captured by Indians and handed over to the British. On his release he settled in Pennsylvania, where he developed his ideas for building a steamboat.

The most remarkable part of the Fitch story is that when he started he had never seen an actual steam engine, only an illustration of a Newcomen engine in a book. How he thought that monstrous machine could ever take to the water is a mystery. He had, however, heard that a man called Watt had made improvements. With this scanty information he designed and built his engine with the help of a clockmaker, Henry Voigt. In 1787 the vessel *Perseverance* was given its trial. It was an extraordinary affair, driven along by banks of three oars, set on either side of the hull, powered by the engine. It was not a great success, and a new version appeared that now had the oars mounted in the stern, paddling along like ducks' feet, similar to the system first tried and soon abandoned by the French duke. In 1790, Fitch had established a regular steamboat service between Philadelphia and Burlington, New Jersey. He had hoped to get a monopoly in steamboat construction, but when that was denied his investors lost faith. Several other attempts to build steamboats in both Europe and America all came to nothing, and his latter years saw him deeply involved in litigation over land he had originally surveyed in Kentucky. When he died in 1798,

The *Clermont*, designed by the American engineer Robert Fulton, was the first paddle steamer to enter into regular service. Built in 1807 it carried passengers on the Hudson River between Albany and New York. Although always known as *Clermont*, it was actually launched under the more prosaic name *North River Steamer*. The photograph shows a replica built in 1909. (*Library of Congress*)

America still had no steamboat services on its rivers and canals and his name slipped into obscurity. Yet he was a man of bold imagination: it is hard to conceive just how difficult it must have been to make any kind of working steam engine without having seen one, let alone one capable of driving a boat. It was the next American inventor who went down in the history books as the first really successful steamboat pioneer.

Robert Fulton was born in Pennsylvania in 1765, the son of Irish immigrants, whose farm failed in 1771. By 1774 his father was dead. After a necessarily brief education, Fulton was apprenticed to a jeweller in Philadelphia, where he showed a talent for painting miniature portraits for lockets. This set him off on a career as an artist and, in 1787, local merchants raised money to send him to London to improve his art. He had a modest success, but the competition was far greater in cosmopolitan London than in the still provincial city of Philadelphia. Nevertheless he stayed in Britain at the start of the Canal Mania years, and developed a new enthusiasm for transport. He wrote a book, advocating a system of short, local canals, linked by inclines, with no locks. The idea was never taken up.

He may have spent ten years in Britain, but in 1797 he moved to France, where he proposed building a new type of vessel to attack the British fleet – a submarine. He even built a craft at his own expense, but it had no effect on naval warfare. But it was in Paris that he met the American minister in France, Robert R. Livingston, who had acquired a monopoly for running steamboats in the state of New York – even though he had no steamboats to run. The two men joined forces to make a steamboat that was tried out on the Seine, using an 8-horse power French engine. It was not entirely successful, but showed enough promise to continue the experiments. By 1804, Fulton was back in London, now trying to sell to the British the idea of building a submarine with which to attack the French. But with the Royal Navy's domination of the seaways there was no interest. So, by 1805, he was back with the original idea of steamboats, this time using a Boulton & Watt engine, which he had shipped back to America in parts.

By 1807 the vessel, originally just known as *Steamboat* but later as the *Clermont*, was ready. The vessel was 150ft long and its single cylinder engine drove paddle wheels on either side of the vessel. Boulton & Watt were still committed to low pressure steam, and the use of a separate condenser, so the wood-burning boiler was only needed to produce steam at a decidedly modest 3 pounds per square inch (psi). On her trial run she completed the 150 mile journey along the Hudson, between Albany and New York in thirty-two hours, which might not seem like rapid progress, but the existing horse-drawn boat service took four days. Modifications were made and by September she was in regular service. The owners of the sloops that had monopolised traffic up to then, were less than pleased by the rival, and a suspiciously large number of 'accidental' encounters occurred between their vessels and the vulnerable paddle wheels. Guards over the wheels alleviated that problem and regular commercial steamboat runs were finally established.

The paddle steamer became a vital link in the American transport system, especially on the Mississippi. In popular imagination the typical Mississippi steamer was a showboat, inhabited by gamblers and ladies of dubious virtue; in reality most of the traffic was the vital carriage of cotton from the fields to the main port of New Orleans. This illustration shows a stern wheeler in which every space has been crammed full of bales of cotton. (*Public Library of Cincinnati & Hamilton County*)

The paddle steamer was ideal for the major rivers of America, and the Mississippi steamers became legendary. Today, we see them as they have appeared in films, as exotic floating pleasure houses where professional gamblers fleeced the unwary. In practice, most of the river traffic was less glamorous. There was an immense trade in the nineteenth century, bringing cotton from the plantations of the South down to New Orleans for shipment to the mills of Lancashire. These boats not only carried cotton in the hold but also bales were heaped up all along the decks, so that the whole vessel looked like a pile of bales on the move. The other passenger boats did and do exist. One of the few Mississippi paddle boats, still actually worked by a steam engine, the *Natchez*, still takes passengers for trips on the river at New Orleans. Along the way they are regaled by music from the steam calliope, an organ in which steam is blown through the pipes instead of air.

Suitable as they might have been for the vast reaches of the Mississippi, American canal authorities were no more enthusiastic than their counterparts on the Forth & Clyde had been. The same problems of the wash eroding the banks led to them being banned. It seemed that steam was destined to be limited first to rivers, then ocean-going vessels or to

Regular steamer services were introduced onto the Göta Canal from an early date. One of these was named after Erik Nordewall, the engineer in charge of the first section of canal linking Gôtenborg to Lake Varna. It sank, but its remains were discovered at the bottom of a lake. Now a full-scale replica of the paddle steamer has been built and steams again on the canal. (*Paddlesteamer, Sweden*)

canals specifically designed to take ships rather than narrow boats and barges. One of the first actual canals to use steam power on the water was the Göta Canal in Sweden. The works that had been started beside the canal at Motala not only built structures for the canal, such as locks and bridges, but also even before it was completed they were building paddle steamers for use on the waterway. The work continued after the canal was opened and one vessel, named after the Swedish engineer, Eric Nordwall, was built in 1835. It foundered twenty years later, but the remains were found and a replica was recently completed. It steams again down the canal.

In Britain, where so much pioneering work had been done on both canals and steam engines, movement towards uniting the two was painfully slow. The major difficulty was with the narrow canals. There was never any question of using side paddles: boats would have been unable to fit into the locks, and stern paddles would have been vulnerable to damage in the locks. Even if that had not been the case, when your boat size is limited you cannot give over extra space for paddle wheels, an engine and its fuel, nor can you pay extra crew to look after the machinery. It was only in the 1860s that steam narrow boats came into limited use, mostly run by the carrying company Fellows, Morton & Clayton (F.M.C.) on the Grand Junction Canal. To save on space, they needed small, powerful engines. By this date, high-pressure engines were common, and these were worked at 140psi, a huge increase from the 3psi of *Clermont*. There was also another factor that made a huge difference. Back in the 1830s an Englishman, Francis Pettit Smith, had devised a

The introduction of steam power to British canals only developed slowly. At the end of the nineteenth century, steam-powered narrow boats were introduced, which worked both as cargo carriers and tugs, hauling an unpowered narrow boat, the butty, behind them. One company that specialised in this type of craft was Fellows, Morton & Clayton and one of their steamers, *Sultan*, is shown here with the crew. To maximise their profits, these boats were worked 'fly' on non-stop runs. (*Waterways Archive Gloucester*)

different way of moving a vessel through water – the screw propeller. It was an immediate success. Brunel changed his plans for his second steamship, the iron–hulled *Great Britain,* abandoning the original paddle wheel design in favour of the screw propeller. The big advantage, as far as use on canals was concerned, was that instead of being stuck either out at the side or behind the stern, as the paddle wheels needed to be, the propeller could be tucked away under a counter stern.

The system worked because the steamer was powerful enough to tow a second narrow boat, the unpowered 'butty' behind it, and the locks on the Grand Junction were wide enough to take in the two vessels side by side. The great advantage the steam engine has over the horse is that it never gets tired, so the boats were run 'fly' travelling day and night. To work to a strict timetable, they had to carry change crews: usually five men on the steamer and three on the butty. Working the steamer must have been an interesting exercise in communication: the steerer couldn't see or control the engine, and the engine driver couldn't see where they were going. Communication was through coded signals on a lanyard. But they were undoubtedly efficient: a timetable for a run from Limehouse

Basin at the end of the Regent's Canal to Fazeley, near Birmingham, was scheduled to take just forty-four hours, during which time the crew would have travelled 151 miles and passed through 161 locks. The men were considered elite and were smartly dressed in white uniforms; not the most practical colour for a coal-fired steamer. One of these craft has been preserved and restored to full working order, and *President* can regularly be seen out on the water in the old FMC livery.

One much appreciated steam innovation on the narrow canals was tugs for tunnels. Many had no towpaths, so the vessels had to be legged through. Life was easier for crews when they could be towed along as part of a string of boats. The only ones who would have regretted their arrivals were the professional leggers, who had done the job at some of the country's longer tunnels.

The main use for steam on British canals was on the broad waterways of the north of England and Scotland. The owners of the Forth & Clyde Canal, having turned their back on the original steam tugs, tried again in the middle of the nineteenth century. They

One very successful use of steam on British canals was tugs to pull narrow boats through tunnels that had no towpaths. This photograph taken c.1910 shows a large number of horse-drawn boats waiting to be towed through Blisworth Tunnel. The tug can just be seen to the left of the picture. At this date the Grand Union had not yet been formed, hence the initials on the tug for the Grand Junction Canal Company. (*Waterways Archive Gloucester*)

installed an engine in an 80 tonne lighter, *Thomas*, and trialled it on the canal in 1856. It was a success and from this simple beginning a distinctive vessel was born – the Clyde Puffer. The popular name was given because in the original version, exhaust steam was sent straight up the funnel, sending out a puff of smoke and steam with every stroke. The vessel was still recognisably derived from the old lighters. It had to be built to fit the locks and maximise the cargo space, so it was flat bottomed, bluff in the bows with a rounded stern. The captain had a cabin aft and the crew had their accommodation in the foc's'le up in the bows. In between there was just one large hold, covered in hatches. Originally there was an open steering position, but this was soon changed with the addition of a wheelhouse immediately behind the funnel. This makes steering interesting. The engine was developed as a compound. That is, steam under high pressure enters one small cylinder, and then exhausts into a second larger cylinder. The difference in size balances out the power – high pressure acting on a small piston, the lower pressure on the larger area. The puffers were soon freed from the confines of the canal and became the workhorses of the

The Forth & Clyde Canal Company had rejected steam at the beginning of the nineteenth century. They finally succumbed by the end of it, introducing small cargo steamers that became known as 'Puffers'. The name derived from the exhaust steam that passed up the funnel with smoke from the boiler in a series of regular puffs. This Puffer was working on the canal in the twentieth century and is seen here loading up with whisky from a warehouse at Port Dundas. In later years the Puffers spread out from the canal, trading up and down the west coast of Scotland and out to the islands. (*Waterways Archive Gloucester*)

Highlands and islands of the Scottish west coast. The little craft were made famous in the
Para Handy tales of the puffer *Vital Spark* and her crew.

Attempts in America to introduce steam on the canals moved at much the same pace
as they had in Britain. Taking one canal as an example, the Chesapeake & Ohio, one
finds a string of trials, failures and false starts. A committee had been set up in 1831 to
examine the whole question, but always with the proviso that nothing could be done
that might damage the banks. Nothing materialised at first. There was, however, one
promising development. Pettit Smith was not the only man working on screw propulsion.
John Ericsson, a Swedish-born engineer who had earlier designed a locomotive in Britain
but then moved to America, had the same idea at much the same time, and one of his craft
was tried on the canal in the 1840s. There was a period of experiment with steam tugs, but
their use was severely limited by rules that they should not travel faster than 4 miles per
hour and not draw more than 4ft of water.

The company was still wrestling with the problem in the 1860s. A report in the *Alleganian*
newspaper on 7 July 1868, after commenting on the fact that 'the several attempts heretofore
made to introduce steam propulsion upon our Canal have proved unsatisfactory', went on
to praise an invention by Captain James L. Catheart. His device had been successfully
tested by the Philadelphia Transportation & Freight Co. It worked 'in such a manner that
the banks of the canal will not be washed away as they are liable to be now by the ordinary

CANAL AQUEDUCT AT MEDFORD, AND STEAMBOAT "MERRIMACK" (THE THIRD
IN MASSACHUSETTS WATERS), 1818.

This illustration shows the steam tug *Merrimack* on the Middlesex Canal at Medford in 1818. It is crossing
the Medford aqueduct over the Mystic River. This appears to be the oldest known record of steam being
used on American canals. They seem, nevertheless, to have been very little used on canals, yet finding
much greater use on rivers and river navigations. (*Middlesex Canal Association*)

screw, which makes so great a commotion in the water that its use is strictly prohibited'. The propeller was attached to a flexible knuckle joint from the drive shaft and also to a rudder, so that both could be moved together –much as a modern outboard motor is swivelled by the tiller. It was claimed that whereas 'the old lumbering boats' were run at a cost of 23 cents a mile, with the new steamers this was cut to 9 cents, and the vessels could move at 6mph without causing damage. The Pennsylvania Company was reported as having changed all their vessels to the new system at a cost of $8,000 per boat.

There was a short period of use of steam packets on the Chesapeake & Ohio canal, but in general the steam engine never had any great impact on canal traffic anywhere in the world. Horses and mules trudged towpaths well into the twentieth century. One type of steam engine, however, did have a huge effect on the canals and that will be the subject of the next chapter.

Chapter 12

The Rival

Early on in the canal age, the Duke of Bridgewater remarked that his canals would 'do well enough if they can keep clear of those damn'd tramways'. Not many agreed with him. The tramways were seen as vital links between industrial sites and waterways, feeding cargo down to the boats. One of the many tramways in South Wales came into being, not so much from the necessity to bring cargo to the canal, but to settle a troublesome dispute. The Glamorganshire Canal was promoted by the iron masters of Merthyr Tydfil to link to the docks in Cardiff. The major shareholder was William Crawshay of the Cyfarthfa ironworks. For a time all went well, but this canal had forty-nine locks in just 24 miles of waterway and as trade grew so did congestion. Crawshay began demanding that, as the main promoter, his craft should be given precedence. Samuel Homfray of the rival Penydarren ironworks had a radical solution. The original Act had allowed for 'collateral cuts or railways' to be built. Homfray decided to circumvent the worst bottleneck on the canal by building a 9½-mile tramway from his works to the canal at Abercynon. It was a conventional tramway, with cast-iron rails set on stone blocks and was worked by horses. It was built on a gentle 1 in 145 gradient, so that horses only hauled the full trucks downhill and had the return journey with empty wagons. It would have remained no more than a footnote to canal history but for events in February 1804.

The start of the new century had seen the end of James Watt's patent and with it his monopoly of steam engine development. Other engineers took up the chance to make new, bold experiments. One of these was the Cornish mining engineer Richard Trevithick. He experimented with high-pressure steam. He realised that he could dispense with the condenser, only losing the effect of atmospheric pressure, just under 15psi. The high-pressure engine could thus be made small enough to be moved around. His first experiments were portable engines that could be hauled by horses to where they were needed. But by 1801 he had built a portable engine that could drive itself along – a locomotive. His first experimental model huffed and puffed its way up Camborne Hill in Cornwall on Christmas Eve of that year, accompanied by a cheering crowd, many of whom climbed on board for the ride. It was destroyed in an accident a few days later. But Trevithick went on to design a steam-powered stagecoach that was demonstrated on the streets of London. It was not greeted with enthusiasm, and was very difficult to steer. The mechanism was simply a tiller attached to a single front wheel. That problem was about to be solved; steam locomotives would run on rails.

Homfray had heard of Trevithick's experiments and suggested that he build a new version to run on his tramway to take over from the horses. The engine was to be dual-purpose. Not only was it expected to run on the tracks, but it also had to work as a stationary engine, powering machinery at the ironworks. In one respect, the trials were a great success. Trevithick wrote to a friend that 'It worked very well and ran up hill and down with great ease, and very manageable, we have plenty of steam and power.' Unfortunately the engine proved too heavy for the brittle cast-iron rails, several of which were smashed. A second Trevithick engine sent up to a coalfield in North-East England suffered a similar fate. The first experiments ended.

There matters rested until 1812, when the costs of the Napoleonic Wars sent the price of fodder for horses soaring. Now it was the owners of the Middleton Colliery near Leeds who were looking to reduce the costs of getting their coal to the Aire & Calder Canal. They were aware of the breaking rails and looked to use a locomotive that would be light enough not to cause damage but with sufficient power to do the work. The solution was a rack and pinion railway, in which a cog on the engine engaged with a toothed rack laid along one side of the conventional rails. The system worked, and attracted considerable attention, particularly from the colliery owners of Northumberland and Durham. This was the world's first successful, commercial railway and other colliery lines soon followed, but advances in technology made it possible to dispense with the cumbersome rack and pinion. That system would later be revived for mountain railways. This phase of railway history culminated in the opening of the Stockton & Darlington railway in 1825. This

The earliest railways were all designed to take coal from collieries to the nearest navigable river or canal and were little different from the earlier tramways, apart from their use of steam locomotives. The illustration shows a section of the Hetton Colliery Railway, opened in 1822. One locomotive is seen hauling a line of trucks down to Staithes on the River Wear. A second engine can be seen at the foot of an incline, used to move trucks up and down the hillside by means of a stationary steam engine; the hill itself is somewhat exaggerated. At this date, many simply regarded railways as being useful means of feeding navigable waterways. (*Anthony Burton*)

has been hailed as an important step towards the modern rail system as it was the first line approved by an Act of Parliament that specified the use of steam locomotives. In its essentials, it was still a colliery line, writ large. Locomotives were only used in taking coal from the various mines to the River Tees. Passengers were carried, but at first they had to make do with a conventional stagecoach pulled by horses, but fitted with flanged wheels to run on the rails.

Up to this point the canal authorities were sanguine about the developments. Thomas Telford argued that railway development was valuable in doing exactly what the tramways had done – bringing goods to canals. He still believed that nothing could improve on water transport for efficiency. If locomotives had never developed beyond the slow, clanking, often unreliable machines of the early days, then he would have been right. But that was never going to be the case: progress was inevitable, and the whole railway scene was transformed in the 1830s with the promotion of the Liverpool & Manchester Railway.

This was a different proposition, directly challenging existing routes, including the pioneering Bridgewater Canal. The situation had more than a touch of irony. Back in the 1760s, the Duke of Bridgewater had met fierce opposition from the established river navigations when he applied for his Act of Parliament, as they claimed they faced ruin if he went ahead. Now it was the turn of the Duke's successors to make a similar claim – that permitting the railway to be built would spell financial disaster to the canals. And just as the Duke had argued that his canal was for the general good and should not be stopped by narrow financial interests and won his case, so now the railway company won a similar argument after a long battle. The canal companies hired the very best lawyers and George Stephenson, the chief engineer, was mercilessly grilled. It became apparent that the initial surveys had been rushed and every flaw was highlighted. The Bill was thrown out and had to be presented all over again – after work had been redone, checked and double-checked. This time the Act was passed.

The Liverpool & Manchester was no mere colliery line, but it took a competition to prove that it could be worked for both goods and passenger traffic using steam locomotives. The winning engine was the famous *Rocket* designed by Robert Stephenson. It was an inter-city line, offering travel at such previously unimaginable speeds as 30mph. And just as the success of the Bridgewater had brought a flurry of Canal Acts in its wake, so now too there was a rush to build main line railways across Britain. Canals were no longer the latest things in the transport world. And, in time, the railway network would spread, first to Europe, then America and eventually across the world. And wherever they appeared the old canal companies had to fight back or capitulate.

One obvious way to compete was to reduce costs. But boats were limited in size by the locks through which they had to pass. Attempts to replace horses by steam power had not proved successful. That only left one area where savings could be made – the cost of the boat crews. Up to now, in Britain, the work of most boatmen had been little different

The first really modern railway, carrying both freight and passengers, hauled by steam locomotives, was the Liverpool & Manchester. In this picture it can be seen crossing the Sankey Navigation, which in its time had been an innovative canal, built before the Bridgewater. Competition proved too much for the Sankey, which became derelict, and anyone visiting the site today would find the viaduct still in use, but the canal little more than a depression in the ground. (*Anthony Burton*)

from that of, for example, a carter. They left home, went to their boats and returned home at the end of a journey. Now, however, the boating community were transformed into watery nomads. Instead of living in conventional houses, they would all have to live on board. On the main network of narrow canals, this would mean everyone squeezing into a cabin in the stern. This was necessarily no wider than the width of the boat, about 7ft, and only slightly longer. Fitting everything into such a space was a masterpiece of design. The cabin contained a range used for both heating and cooking and a cupboard for stores. The latter had a door that folded down alongside a bench to create a double bed. It would have been a spartan living space if the boat families had not made it bright and cheerful. Brasses were always highly polished, and the boatwomen were famous for their crochet work, producing lace curtains, matched by spotless lace-edged plates. It was probably in this period that canal narrow boats developed their traditional decoration of painted roses and castles. They may have given up their homes on land, but at least they could take grand homes and flourishing gardens around with them, even if they were only painted.

As railways developed they claimed many canal victims. This milepost is one of the few remains now seen of the Oakham Canal. Begun with great enthusiasm in the 1790s, it singularly failed to show a profit and it was with great relief rather than regret that the company sold the whole concern to the Midland Railway. The railway company promptly closed it as it obstructed plans for their rapidly developing system.

The facilities on the boats were strictly limited. Every boat carried its decorated buckie can in which to collect fresh water for drinking and cooking, but washing relied on water from the canal. E. Temple Thurston, in his classic 1911 account of a canal trip on a narrow point, asked the accompanying boatman about the toilet arrangements: 'Why, look you, sur – that hedge which runs along by every tow-path. If Nature couldn't grow enough leaves on that hedge to hide a sparrow's nest, it ain't no good to God, man nor beast.'

There were two advantages to moving on board the boat. The most obvious was that families no longer needed to rent a house on land. The second was that the boatman now had a crew who didn't ask for wages. Everyone was expected to do their bit, even the children. They learned to lead the horse along the towpath from an early age. Nellie Cartwright began her boating life in the first years of the twentieth century and she told her story to actors from the Mikron Theatre Company, who were researching a show about boat people. She remembered one incident, when the family took the boat through Braunston tunnel on the Grand Junction one early morning. She was taking the horse in the pitch dark to rejoin the rest of the family as they legged through. She was cold and frightened, but the horse kept muzzling her: 'I thought to myself, "He's telling me not to be afraid," and when I got to the end of the tunnel, I was as brave as brave.' It was a hard life. As a grown woman she regularly loaded and unloaded up to 30 tonnes of cargo by hand, but she never objected. Her happiest memories were of the peaceful journeys, with the quiet, plodding horse. It is a life few of us can imagine, of unremitting hard work and an almost total lack of essential comforts, yet in her own words, 'I would do it again exactly the same as I had it with the horses, the boats, the loading.'

It was often easy to make a comparison between the new railways and the older canals. When Robert Stephenson surveyed the line for a railway to connect London to Birmingham, he selected a route very close to that chosen by Jessop for the Grand Junction Canal. The illustration must have been made very early in the history of the line as it appears to show the train hauled by one of the early Planet Class locomotives. (*Anthony Burton*)

Little more could be done in the short term to help the narrow boat community compete with the railways. Their greatest problem was the size of the boats and the loads that could be carried: what had seemed more than adequate in the 1760s, when the only competition came from packhorses or lumbering carts staggering down poorly surfaced roads, looked less appealing in the middle of the nineteenth century. The situation was not quite the same on the broad canals. The Aire & Calder Company had shown a rare willingness to move with the times. The waterway had an even longer history than that of the Brindley era canals, work having started as far back as 1699. In the early nineteenth century, what was in effect a new canal was built from the Aire at Knottingley, just outside Castleford, to a new port on the Ouse at Goole. The engineer in charge was John Rennie, and the canal opened in 1826, just six years after the passing of the Act. Until the arrival of the canal, Goole was just a hamlet of scattered houses. Now it grew into a considerable town. In 1828 the Company issued a statement to the press extolling the magnificence of the new port. It was now, they declared, 'placed on a footing of equality with those of London, Dublin and Liverpool, and of superiority to all others in the United Kingdom, warehouses of special security being to be found in none other.' They referred to the provision of secure, bonded warehouses, still a rarity at that time.

The arrival of railway competition in Britain resulted in boatmen having to abandon houses on the land and live with their families on the boats. Whole families were able to squeeze into the back cabin of a narrow boat, including children such as these. At least by the time the picture was taken, motor boats had been introduced, so there were two cabins: one in the motor and the other on this, the unpowered boat, the butty. (*Waterways Archive Gloucester*)

Visitors to modern day Goole will find it difficult to reconcile what they find with this enthusiastic description. The notice also added another advantage found at Goole: 'A steam towing boat, called the *Britannia* of 50 horse power, is provided to facilitate the navigation of the Rivers Humber and Ouse.'

The Aire & Calder continued under the leadership of their chief engineer, William Bartholomew, who oversaw improvements in the navigation and also introduced a new

To compete with the railways, canals were modernised in many different ways. On the Aire & Calder Navigation this included a new type of vessel, known as a 'Tom Pudding'. Looking, as the name suggests, like outsize pudding tins, these could be linked and towed by a tug. Here they are seen being loaded with coal at a colliery site, from where they would be taken to the port of Goole for transhipment. (*Waterways Archive Gloucester*)

type of water transport. In 1863 he designed compartment boats, which were little more than oblong boxes that could be joined together in chains of up to fifteen vessels, for haulage by a steam tug. The first vessel in the line was fitted with dummy bows to make the train more manageable. Their similarity to pudding tins earned them the name 'Tom Puddings', a name that stuck as long as they remained in use. They were designed to bring coal from the Yorkshire collieries to Goole. At the port, the individual Tom Puddings were brought under massive hoists, where they were lifted to the top of the tower, upended and the coal poured down chutes to the holds of waiting ships.

The system was so effective that it remained in use well into the second half of the twentieth century. The author saw the system in operation during a trip on the Aire & Calder in the 1970s and waited while they came down the lock. The train was clearly too long to fit into the lock. The hawsers that held the train to the tug were pulled in and the tug passed into the lock, taking the first seven containers with it. That left another eight apparently stranded and tugless. The answer was simple. The lock was refilled and then, with the top gates opened, the bottom paddles were raised. The flow of water was strong

At Goole the Tom Puddings were unloaded by being floated under a hoist, lifted to the top and upended, allowing the coal to flow down a chute into a waiting ship. Although no longer in use, this hoist has been preserved as an important industrial monument. (*Anthony Burton*)

enough to suck in the rest of the containers. It was thanks to this programme of constant improvement that the Aire & Calder survived railway competition for so long. Other waterways were less fortunate.

Many of the canals built during the mania years had struggled to make a profit even before the railways came along. The Oakham Canal is a classic example. For the shareholders, however, the railways were a boon. The canal lay right in the path required by the Midland Railway, which simply bought it up, closed it down and built on top of it. For the first time the investors actually got money back after half a century of losses. Other canals were bought up, but kept open. The Great Western Railway, for example, bought several canals, including the Kennet & Avon. In several places, the lines of rails and waterway lie close together, and the railway company was not in favour of too much competition. They were required by an Act of Parliament to keep the canal open, but that didn't mean they had to encourage its use. They took their cue from the poet Arthur Hugh Clough and his advice to doctors:

'Thou shalt not kill; but need'st not strive
   Officiously to keep alive.'

Another inevitable result of the coming of the railways was that investors lost interest in canals. They were now seen as out of date, and investors poured their money into the new transport system. Across the Atlantic, canal companies put up a spirited fight – even though it was a canal company that tried to introduce railways in the first place.

The first commercial experiments with steam locomotives in America began on the portage section of the Hudson & Delaware Canal as it crossed the hills. As no one in America had any experience of designing and building locomotives, the company sent their engineer, Horatio Allen, to England. He brought back four engines, one of which designed by John Urpeth Rastrick at his works at Stourbridge had an embossed lion's head on the end of the boiler, earning it the name *Stourbridge Lion*. This locomotive was tested, and Allen manned the footplate for the first run in August 1829. On his own admission he had 'never run a locomotive nor any other engine before'. But, he added, 'If there is any danger in this ride, it is not necessary that more than one should be subjected to it.' The section chosen for the trial began with a straight section of about 200 yards, then crossing a trestle bridge over the Lackawaxen Creek, before heading off on a curved track into the woods.

'The locomotive having no train behind it answered at once to the movement of the valve; soon the straight line was run over, the curve (and trestle) was reached and passed before there was time to think … and soon I was out of sight in the three miles' ride in the woods of Pennsylvania.'

What Allen didn't realise as he bowled cheerfully along was that the spectators had seen the wooden bridge sway alarmingly as he crossed it and that the heavy engine was leaving mangled and twisted rails in its wake. The experiment was a failure; the lion had roared its last and was dumped in a shed where it was left to rot. It was inevitable, however, that as both engines and tracks improved, a railway system would be developed in America and challenge the canals and waterways for their trade.

The first real competition was felt by the Erie Canal as railways encroached on their territory. First on the scene was the Mohawk & Hudson Company, which laid lines between Albion and Schenectady. The first locomotive to work the line was the rather ungainly *Dewitt Clinton*. It was a mark of the growing confidence in American railroads that this was designed and built in America, not imported from Britain. It must have been galling to the canal company that the designer, John Bloomfield Jervis, was originally engineer to the Delaware & Hudson Canal. Old allegiances were already being broken. It made its first run in 1834, proceeding at a stately 15mph on the flat, but struggling with hills. Nevertheless, it was sufficiently successful for other companies to follow. By 1847 there were ten independent railroads working along the same basic line of the Erie Canal. Had they co-operated, they might have posed more of a threat, but they were too busy competing to worry about boats. The different companies built their own termini and refused to pass on details of their schedules, so that although in theory it was possible to travel between Buffalo and Albany in about 14 hours, the wise traveller would allow at least a couple of days. Charles F. Carter described such a journey in his book *When the Railroads were New*. His account tells of delays, including a wait at Syracuse that lasted all day, during which time no one dared leave the train in case it left without them. In the event it took 38½ hours to cover the 290 miles – an average speed of just over 7mph, which must have made a leisurely trip on a canal packet appealing.

Freight traffic was not hugely affected at first, largely because the canal offered lower rates. But in spite of the teething difficulties of the railroad companies, the canal companies took the threat to their revenues seriously and waged a propaganda war, portraying it as a threat to life and limb. Inevitably, just as in Britain, investors moved money away from canal construction and into railroad building. And, again, it was the smaller canals that suffered first: five of the lesser canals in New York State succumbed quickly, and the Delaware & Hudson bowed to the inevitable and rebranded itself the Delaware & Hudson Railroad. The Erie fared better than most, but the development of the New York Central Railroad in 1853, which united the old mix of lines in a single company, proved a formidable rival. Eventually the Erie went the way of all the other American canals as traffic dwindled and closure became inevitable.

Railways spread rapidly through mainland Europe in the 1830s, although they reached some parts surprisingly late: Spain didn't get a line until 1848, and Portugal, Sweden and Norway had to wait until the 1850s. Russia, however, was among the early pioneers.

American canals also suffered from railway competition, as is dramatically illustrated by this photograph. It shows barges below Lock 38 on the Chesapeake & Ohio Canal. There has obviously been either a breach or a severe drought and they are unable to move. In the background is the imposing trestle railway viaduct over which trains can run unimpeded. (*Chesapeake & Ohio Canal Society*)

The immediate effects were not so dramatic as they had been in Britain, where investors had almost instantly favoured the new system. In France, Marc Seguin had designed a locomotive to work the Lyon & St. Etienne Railway, which had previously used horses, as early as 1828, and new lines were soon being built, intended from the first for steam locomotives. Yet French enthusiasm for canals had not diminished, largely because they were built on far more generous lines than the narrow canals that dominated the British scene. Even as new railways were being planned and built, important canal projects were also getting under way.

The Canal du Midi had been a great success, but as a route from the Mediterranean the canalised section only extended as far as Toulouse where it joined the Garonne. The river was difficult to navigate, prone to dropping levels in summer and flooding in winter. In 1838 a new canal to bypass the problem area was authorised. The Canal Lateral à la Garonne was begun in 1839 and completed in 1856. It was a massive undertaking, running for 194km from Toulouse to enter the tidal river at Casters-en-Dorthe. It was built on an impressive scale, with fifty-three locks, able to take vessels 30m long and 5.5m wide. There are two imposing aqueducts: over the Tarn, near Moissac, and across the Garonne at Agen. The latter is the more impressive, 539m long and carried on twenty-three masonry arches. Recently the canal has been improved, with locks being increased in size to take 240 tonne barges.

180. Berlin.
Hochbahn, Anhalter Bahn, Landwehrkanal.

In Germany, canal construction continued into the railway age. The Landwehr Canal was built in 1845, forming, with the River Spree, a loop around Berlin. When it came to building the section of the city's underground railway system – the S-Bahn that ran above ground – it was found convenient to build it over the line of the old canal. This section has changed little over the years, but the line seen carrying a steam locomotive no longer exists.

There was a bottleneck at the locks at Montech, and it was decided to bypass them by a novel device, a water slope, built in 1874. A boat approaching the slope to make the trip downhill floats up against a watertight gate, situated a little way down the slope. Once the boat is in position, the gate is moved by two locomotives, one on each side of the slope. As it travels down, the wedge of water with the boat floating in it is also carried down to the bottom of the slope. When that is reached, the gate is lifted and the boat can carry on with its journey. For an uphill journey, the boat floats up to the slope, and the gate closes behind it.

Even more ambitious was the building of the Canal de la Marne au Rhin, which became France's longest canal at 310km, with 171 locks and a number of tunnels, including the 4,877m Mauvages and the 2,307m Arzviller. It proved a very important waterway and a commercial success, linking Strasbourg to the busy industrial regions of Alsace Lorraine. It also demonstrated the French view that both railways and canal were important in an integrated transport system. Work on building the canal began in 1846 and at the same time construction got under way on a railway on the same route, the two often running side by side.

Germany also continued building canals into the railway age. Berlin doubled in size during the first half of the nineteenth century, as the capital of Prussia, and such rapid

Today the Landwehr Canal has become busy with tourist boats, and among the attractions are the many ornate bridges along the way, including this one in Kreutzberg, near the canal basin. (*Anthony Burton*)

growth needed better transport, which was initially met by a new canal network. The city sits on either bank of the River Spree. In 1845 work started on the Landwehr canal that bypassed part of the river and allowed barges to bring vital supplies, especially coal to the developing society and its new industries. It is only 10.5km long, with just two locks, but it had a large port at the centre in what is now the district of Kreutzberg. Where most canals show a certain uniformity in the bridges that cross them, the canal has an enormous variety in every material from brick to iron. Although commercial traffic is scant, it has a booming tourist trade: passengers can enjoy the sites of Berlin by taking the round trip by river and canal. It was the start of a period of development that lasted into the 1870s, linking Berlin to the River Oder. Ironically the canal also proved useful later, when Berlin needed a new urban transport system. These were the underground U-Bahn and above ground S-Bahn. It was difficult fitting rails into an already crowded city without demolishing expensive property. But the canal already cut a swathe through the buildings, so it made sense to run overhead lines directly above the waterway.

Ludwig I of Bavaria, not to be confused with the 'mad king' Ludwig II, was very progressive. He encouraged the development of modern industries and transport. During his reign, the country got its first steam railway, worked initially by a locomotive provided by the Robert Stephenson works in Newcastle, *Der Adler* (The Eagle). The engine is a rare survivor of the early days of European railways. Even before that date he had planned for a waterway that would connect the Main and the Danube. The survey of the line was begun in 1828 and completed in 1832, which seems long, but this was to be a 172km long waterway, with a summit level 110m above the point where it joined the Regnitz, a tributary of the Main. This involved 100 locks, as well as extensive earthworks. Construction began in 1836 and at one time there were some 6,000 men at work. The only mechanical aid was a steam shovel that was used in a deep cutting near Dörlbach. Designed to take 100 tonne barges, it prospered from its opening in 1845 and was soon recording tonnages of almost 200,000 tonnes a year. Inevitably it suffered from railway competition and, with a summit over 450m above sea level, had frequent problems with water shortages. It continued in use for just over a century, by which time work had already begun on an alternative waterway along a similar route. The Rhine-Main-Danube Canal took even longer to complete

The 1840s also saw the construction of the very ambitious 172km long Ludwig's Canal in Germany. Considerable engineering works were needed, including the deep cutting at Dörlbach shown here, with locks able to take 100 tonne barges.

than the Ludwig: begun in 1921, it finally opened throughout in 1992. Further north in Sweden, there was one notable addition to the watery system, joining Lake Vänern to the Norwegian border. Completed in 1868, it arrived only twelve years after the country's first railway.

Railways were also late arriving in Asia: India only got its first line in 1853, but the nineteenth century did see major advances in water transport. There may have been no rush towards steam railways, but the Raj showed a greater enthusiasm for steam on the water. The first paddle steamer was built at Lucknow in 1819 by William Trickett, although the actual engine had to be brought over from the Butterley ironworks in England. By 1834 the powerful East India Company had begun regular services on the Ganges between Calcutta (now Kolkata) and Allahabad. It was a curious service. The side-paddle steamers also carried sail, but were strictly limited to cargo: passengers were housed in a flat-bottomed vessel towed along behind. One hopes it was comfortable as the whole journey could take up to four weeks. The most important company founded in the early days was the India General Steam Navigation Company, established in 1844. Fifteen years later they had a fleet of ten steamers.

India had an extensive system of irrigation canals, dating back to the Mughal period. Over the years, many had fallen into disrepair. One of these was the Doab Canal that ran for 140 miles from the Jumna River in the foothills of the Himalayas. The job of rebuilding it was given to army officers Captain Robert Smith and a 23-year-old artillery officer, Proby Cautley. The work was completed in 1830 when Smith left, leaving Cautley in charge of the works. By 1831 he had been appointed superintendent of canals for the North-Western Provinces. Five years later, he conceived a far grander project – an irrigation canal that would leave the Ganges above Hardwar, and after Nanu would split into two branches, one returning to the Ganges, the other joining the Jumna. This was construction on a vast scale, with the main lines originally planned as running for 255 miles with 73 miles of branches: this was later extended even further and, when completed, the main was 348 miles long. He spent six months going over the ground in 1840, but could only get agreement for its construction with the proviso that it should also be a navigable canal. Work began on the Ganges Canal in 1843, under Cautley's direction.

His first task was to persuade the local Hindu priests to approve the scheme. At first they were bitterly opposed to a dam that would imprison the holy waters of the Ganges, but Cautley appeased them by leaving a gap through which water could flow downstream. He also promised to repair several of the ghats where the pious came to bathe in the river and, at the opening ceremony, prayers were offered up to Lord Ganesh, the god of good beginnings.

Cautley's biggest problem was getting the raw materials he needed, especially bricks. These all had to be made by hand, and he was soon employing contractors with a workforce of nearly a thousand brick moulders and several hundred more to transport the bricks.

Irrigation canals were common in India in the nineteenth century, but the Ganges Canal was a grand undertaking that was designed for navigation as well as water supply. The painting shows the head of the canal near Haridwar in northern India, close to the border with China. It was painted in 1860, just four years after the canal opened.

His attempts to modernise production met fierce opposition: his brickmaking machines were attacked and the men went on strike. The problem was eventually sorted, but the project depended on manual labour. Apart from building dams and digging the channel, at Roorkee, the canal had to be carried over the Ganges on a quarter-mile long aqueduct. The work was eventually completed in 1854.

The grand opening ceremony saw the sluices opened by the Lieutenant-Governor to the accompaniment of a gun salute and the national anthem. Cautley was allowed to retire from the service and when the vessel on which he travelled to join his ship for England passed Fort William, he was given a thirteen-gun salute in honour of his achievement. He received more formal recognition that year, with a knighthood and elevation to the honorary rank of Colonel. When in 1858, the government of India passed to the crown, Cautley was appointed to the fifteen-strong council that ruled under the secretary of state.

The Ganges Canal was not the only navigable canal in India, but it was by far the most significant. Not only did it provide a valuable transport route, but it also succeeded in its prime objective to supply water to 1,500 villages. There was one other long-term effect. Cautley was acutely aware of the lack of engineering expertise in the country, and helped to set up a College of Civil Engineering at Roorkee. It also showed that canals still had value in the railway age.

Chapter 13

A Final Flourish

Many thought that once the railway age had got under way, most canals would be considered anachronistic and ideas for new canal construction would be placed back on the shelf. But a new demand appeared thanks to another development in steam. The early steamships were, like the sailing ships, built of wood, which limited their size. However, Brunel had demonstrated that steam could be used successfully on Atlantic crossings – and that large ships were more economical than small vessels. He developed the iron ship driven by a propeller, the SS *Great Britain*. It ushered in a new age of large vessels and opened up new routes for steamers. But even the biggest ships had a problem on long voyages: stopping to refuel, so anything that could shorten distances was welcome. One busy route took ships between Europe and Asia and involved the long journey round the tip of Africa at Cape Horn. The obvious answer was a shortcut, through the narrow strip of land that separated the Red Sea from the Mediterranean. It was not a new idea.

As mentioned in Chapter 1, the first such canal had begun under the pharaohs, but had fallen into disuse. The canal built by Darius was restored some three centuries later by Ptolemy II in the third century BC, abandoned again and rebuilt once more by the Romans under Trajan (98–117 AD). Once again it was abandoned and once again restored by Amro Ibn Elass in the seventh century AD, partly for shipping grain and also to help devout Muslims reach the Holy Land. It was closed a century later to prevent a threatened invasion of Egypt. After these stops and starts, the project was abandoned for a thousand years.

The idea of a canal was resurrected when Napoleon invaded Egypt. He saw a possible canal as frustrating the British by giving the French better access to Asian markets. Work got under way under the engineer Charles Le Père, but he seriously overestimated the difference in levels between the two seas. His calculations showed the Red Sea as being a massive 10m higher than the Mediterranean and warned that the canal would have a devastating effect in draining water from the one to the other. So, yet another attempt at permanently creating the link failed, but not for long.

In 1833 a French group known as the Saint-Simonians, followers of the teachings of the Comte de Saint-Simon, who argued for a world based on industrialisation and scientific advance, arrived in Egypt. They looked again at the canal idea, but had not made much progress when plague hit Cairo. Several of the group died and the rest hurried back to France. They had, however, discussed their ideas with a young consular official, Ferdinand de Lesseps, and he in turn had talked it over with his friend Sa'id Pasha, the son of the Turkish Viceroy, Muhammad Ali. Nothing was done immediately, but the notion stayed with de Lesseps, even though he was posted away from Egypt in 1839.

The Saint-Simonians had also kept their ideas alive. In 1846 they formed an Association to carry out a formal study of the possibility of building the canal. A new engineering survey showed that the huge difference in levels between the two ends that had caused the abandonment of the Napoleonic proposal simply did not exist. There was no longer any sound engineering reason for not going ahead, but there were political objections. The British raised objections and Muhammad Ali showed little enthusiasm for the project. So once again everything came to a standstill. But a political change then revived it. In 1854 de Lesseps returned to Egypt as Consul where his old friend Sa'id Pasha was the new Viceroy. There was finally momentum and in 1858 La Compagnie Universelle du Canal Maritime du Suez was formed with authority to build the canal and run it for 99 years, after which ownership would revert to the Egyptian government. de Lesseps was given overall control.

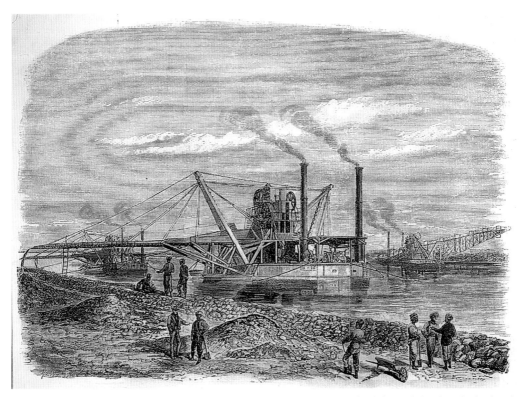

Dredgers on the Suez Canal. Construction work began by cutting, often through hard rock, by hand. Once a sufficient depth had been excavated, water could be introduced and the dredgers floated in to deepen the channel. Material is being dug up from the bottom and the spoil is then being transferred to the bank via the long arm.

Earlier ship canals such as the Göta and the Caledonian had been built on modest lines, never intended for anything bigger than sailing ships. There was never any intention of making the Suez Canal available to sail, simply because the prevailing winds blew in just one direction for most of the year. This would be a canal for steamers, which would be reflected in the size of the operation. It was decided to make the canal one way, with a few passing places, but even so according to the original estimates more than two and a half million cubic metres of material would have to be removed, two million of that by dredging. Fortunately this was an age when new technologies made the task easier than it would have been for a previous generation of engineers.

Large steam-powered bucket dredgers were available as well as a new device, the suction dredger invented by Henri Bazin. A rotating harrow was lowered beneath the bows. This was used to loosen the material on the bed. Water jets mixed the material into a semi-liquid form so that as the vessel moved forward, it could be sucked up by tubes in the stern. It was claimed that the dredger could remove as much as 3,000 cubic metres a day from depths down to 8m to 12m. The dredgers were adapted for the different types of material met in building the canal. For soft rock, steel claws replaced the harrow used for dredging sandy material. Harder rock was broken up by rams with chisel pointed ends. These were monstrous machines: one had ten pointed rams, each 42ft long and weighing 4 tonnes. They were lifted by hydraulic power and allowed to drop onto the rock from heights of up to 20ft, at a rate of more than 200 blows an hour. There were five to each side of the dredger's well and the debris was removed by a bucket dredger, operated by a four-cylinder steam engine. Some of the dredgers had chutes that reached to the shore to carry away the waste. The longest stretched for 60m, and was given extra support by means of posts resting on a barge.

In spite of all this high-tech equipment, there was still an immense workforce needed. Here, employment was little different from the slave labour used by the pharaohs. It was based on the *corvée*, a system of forced labour. It was thought that tens of thousands were brought in every month, but the death toll was horrific.

The canal itself is lock free, running from Port Said on the Mediterranean to Suez to the Red Sea and uses natural features along the way, notably the Great Bitter Lake. It could take the biggest vessels then afloat, with a depth of 8m, although it has subsequently been enlarged several times. The canal itself is 164km long and it reduced the distance for a journey from Britain to India by 7,000km.

The opening of the canal in 1868 was very grand, with convoys of ships setting off from either end, meeting in the middle at the bypass. The ceremony was attended by heads of state and dignitaries and all seemed set for a prosperous future. But the huge debts run up during construction, when the actual costs were double the original estimates, put a severe financial strain on the operation. The Egyptian government that held more than 40 per cent of the shares sold them to the British government in 1875. The story of the Suez

The Suez Canal at Port Said shortly after its opening in 1869. Much has changed over the years, but the prominent tower of the old lighthouse has survived.

Canal is as much about political wranglings as about engineering problems, a state of affairs that existed well into the second half of the twentieth century. Today it belongs to Egypt, where the authorities finished a major new development in 2015 that involved completing 35km of new canal and dredging another 37km to allow larger vessels to use the waterway. After so many stops and starts over the years, it is good news that one scheme at least was completed with no real troubles: in fact, although scheduled to take three years it was finished in just one – a rare accomplishment for any major engineering project.

Although nominally in charge of the Suez project, de Lesseps was no engineer. His role was largely political, reconciling the parties and countries involved and ensuring there was enough money to finish the works. But to most Frenchmen he was the Man of Suez, so when a scheme was put forward for another ship canal through the Isthmus of Panama, the narrow neck of land joining North and South America, he seemed the obvious choice for the job. An international congress was held in Paris in 1879 and two years later work began with de Lesseps in charge. He was then 76 years old and he was helped by his son Charles. The plan was for a lock-free canal like that at Suez, even though it would have to be cut through the rocky spine of the country, which at its highest point was 110m above sea level.

The scheme proved disastrous almost from the start. A huge workforce was recruited largely from the West Indies, but they suffered from disease, mostly malaria and yellow fever. Such fatal conditions were the result of infestation by insects, but no one knew which insects nor how to deal with them. The one 'preventive' measure taken was to stand the feet of beds in tins full of water to prevent insects crawling up. They could not have done anything worse. We now know that the problem was not crawling insects but mosquitoes, and the stagnant water under the beds proved the perfect breeding ground. The well-intentioned authorities had made matters worse and there was an appalling loss of life. An estimated 17,000 Caribbean workers died and some 5,000 French workers. Many engineers supervising the work died too, and others simply decided that life on the canal was too dangerous and headed back to France.

Even without the grim death toll, the work could hardly have gone forward. The decision to build a sea-level canal was always flawed. de Lesseps may have thought it was obvious that he could duplicate the success of Suez, but there is a big difference between constructing a waterway through the flat sands of a desert and building it through rocky hills and jungle. He had convinced the congress set up to review the proposals to accept his plans, largely because of the 136 delegates only 42 were engineers. There was also the difficult question of what should be done about the Chagres River that was likely, if left unchecked, to flood the canal in the rainy season. The scheme was essentially doomed.

Construction finally got under way at the beginning of 1881 with a labour force of some 40,000 men. It struggled on until 1887, when de Lesseps finally admitted that the original plan would not work, and they would have to build locks. The change was made, but it was too late. By 1889 some 900 million francs had been spent, slightly more than the original estimate for the whole project, and only two fifths of the work had been done. The company was bankrupt. It was a national scandal and there were strong indications of corruption. Opponents of the French government then in power demanded that someone's head should roll. The scapegoat was de Lesseps. He was charged with mismanagement, but his son took full responsibility to save his aged father from imprisonment. Charles was found guilty and served a year in prison. A new company was set up to salvage something for the investors, but the best they could do was to bring in a small workforce to ensure that what had been completed did not deteriorate. The favourite solution was to find a buyer for the enterprise that was offered at 430 million francs ($109 million). America was the only likely purchaser, but apart from baulking at the price tag, some American engineers had other ideas about where and how the canal should be built.

What followed was an intense political struggle. There was a strong movement in America for making a canal, spurred on by an event in the Spanish-American war. The US had a naval base in Cuba, but when one of their battleships there was attacked and sunk in 1898, the only other battleship available was stationed in San Francisco and it took 72 days for it to complete the voyage round Cape Horn. With a canal, the trip would have taken a fraction of the time. However, a powerful faction favoured the canal project, but with a wholly new route through Nicaragua. Others wanted a route through Panama, then part of Colombia. Among those in favour of the latter was the distinguished civil engineer George Shattuck Morison, but oddly one of the decisive factors in persuading the US Senate to vote for the Panama route was a postage stamp. Each of the Senators was sent a Nicaraguan stamp showing a local volcano erupting: not the best advert for a spot in which to build a canal. Having agreed the route, all they then had to do was get permission from the Colombian government. They refused.

President Theodore Roosevelt, an enthusiastic supporter of the scheme, was infuriated. He lent his support – and a threatening American military presence – to the movement for

The photograph gives an excellent idea of the scale of operations during the building of the Panama Canal. As the excavations advanced through the rocky terrain of the Culebra Cut, they were followed by rail tracks at three levels, linked by inclined planes, allowing the spoil to be removed quickly and efficiently. (*Library of Congress*)

Panama's independence. Panama duly appeared as a new state in 1903, and had little option other than to grant the US sovereignty over a 10-mile strip of their new country, the Canal Zone. America paid the French for the work they had done and the equipment left behind. The French venture may have ended in failure, but they had excavated some 60 million cubic metres, of which 14 million was from the deep Culebra Cut. The Americans valued everything at $40 million, less than half the original asking price, and the French had little choice. It was that or nothing.

The Americans began work in 1904. Among the first to arrive on the scene were the medical team. Research had shown that mosquitoes carried the diseases, and the Chief Sanitary Officer, Dr William Gorgas, set about dealing with the problem. The yellow fever vector was comparatively easy to eradicate, but the malarial mosquito proved more resistant. It was described as being like 'fighting the beasts of the jungle'. Methods used included draining swamps, introducing species that fed on the larvae of the mosquitoes and spraying poisons around the areas where the mosquitoes bred. There were still deaths from malaria but fatalities were measured in hundreds rather than thousands. This helped persuade Caribbean workers that it was now safe to work in the area and also protected essential skilled staff.

Building the canal was an immense operation in which railways played a key role, together with an array of mechanical excavators. The French had built a rail line that the chief engineer, John F. Stevens, realised was inadequate. The country was unable to provide the necessary food, housing and facilities for the huge workforce, so everything had to be imported and moved along the line of the canal by rail. The same railway had to supply equipment to the workings and carry away the spoil. To make this system more efficient, subsidiary lines were built at different levels within the cuttings. All equipment from rails to locomotives was brought in by sea and American railway workers had to both assemble everything themselves and then run the railway. When work got under way on the deep Culebra cutting that ran through the continental divide, there were some 6,000 men at work drilling holes into the rock and packing them with dynamite. So much material was removed that at times as many as 160 spoil trains a day were running from the site.

The Panama Canal involved work on a scale never attempted before. The French plans had been ambitious, but the Americans found them inadequate. Once the decision had been taken to build locks it was decided to make them even bigger than originally designed. There were to be three sets of locks, built in pairs, set side by side. There was a two-lock flight at Miraflores, followed by a single pair at Pedro Miguel, raising the canal from the Pacific to Gotun Lake, and the Gotun locks then lowered the canal down to the Atlantic. Each lock was 1,050ft long and 110ft wide. Where locks on earlier canals had been built from brick or stone, these locks were concrete. Their construction represents one of the greatest civil engineering feats of the time.

A lock under construction on the Panama Canal. The workers are dwarfed by the immense lock gates. (*Library of Congress*)

Stevens, who had done so much both to promote and plan the canal, resigned in 1907 on unspecified personal grounds and Roosevelt replaced him with a military man, Lieutenant Colonel George Washington Goethals. He made it clear that he was not going to run a conventional military campaign: 'I now consider that I am commanding the Army of Panama, and that the enemy we are going to combat is the Culebra Cut and the locks and dams at both ends of the Canal, and any man who does his duty will never have any cause to complain of militarism.' To emphasis the point, he never wore uniform while at work on the canal.

The work was finally completed in 1914 and although Goethals was the man in charge, he always gave full credit to the careful planning of his predecessor Stevens. The honours are rightly shared.

Britain also acquired a new ship canal at the end of the nineteenth century. Although it could not match either the Suez or the Panama for scale, it did also use the latest technology. The waterway was to provide a direct link from the Mersey to Manchester for vessels up to 15,000 tonnes, but allowance was made for smaller craft. Locks were duplicated: the large are 600ft by 65ft, with two pairs of intermediate gates, so that the length could be

The biggest problem facing the engineers building the Panama Canal was cutting through the hills of the continental divide at Culebra. The photograph shows SS *Kentuckian* being towed through the cutting, with a dredger close to the bank. (*Library of Congress*)

shortened; the small, relatively speaking, are 235ft by 18ft, again with intermediate gates. We know a lot about the construction, largely because this was the age when engineers produced detailed statistics. The official handbook of 1894 recorded that 76 million tonnes of spoil had been shifted, of which 20 per cent was rock; the building materials were recorded as well: 175,000 cubic yards of brick, 220,000 cubic yards of masonry and 1,250,000 cubic yards of cement.

The huge mass of material removed and the extensive construction work was only possible because of technology that was not available in the earlier canal age. More than 100 steam excavators were used and some 200 cranes. Spoil was removed by wagons running on 223 miles of railway track and hauled by 173 locomotives. Yet in spite of this, the canal still relied on about 16,000 navvies. Some things may have improved over the years, but the life of the navvies had changed little. They still lived in makeshift shanty towns and did the most arduous work, such as clearing the spoil and throwing it into the high-sided trucks. In essence, it was little different from the work when digging deep cuttings for railways.

If not on the scale of the Panama Canal, the building of the Manchester Ship Canal also introduced the latest in mechanical aids, such as this mechanical steam excavator. Here too railways were laid to remove the spoil. (*Waterways Archive Gloucester*)

In spite of the extensive use of machines, much of the work of building the Manchester Ship canal was down to the navvies. Their job was to load spoil into the railway trucks by hand. Essentially their work was little different from what it had been when the first canals were being built more than a century earlier. (*Waterways Archive Gloucester*)

The Manchester Ship Canal in its heyday, when it was busy with traffic of all kinds, from ocean-going steamers to barges being towed by a tug. (*Waterways Archive Gloucester*)

The similarity to railway work was underlined by the appointment of Thomas Walker as the main contractor. He had worked on one of the most impressive engineering feats of the railway age – the building of the tunnel under the River Severn.

The new canal cut across existing road systems, so it needed moveable bridges, worked by hydraulics. The new canal also swallowed up the old Irwell Navigation, and here there was a new problem. It was crossed by Brindley's Barton aqueduct that was never designed to let ships pass underneath. It had to go and, instead of a swing bridge, it was replaced by a swing aqueduct. This consists of an iron trough, 18ft wide and mounted on 235ft long girders. The whole structure is carried on roller bearings, supported on a central pier. The two ends can be sealed off, so that when a ship approaches, it can be swung, full of water, through ninety degrees to align with the banks, allowing space for ships to pass either side of the central island. It is very impressive and still works beautifully: I could scarcely see a drop of water being lost from the trough.

Work on the canal began in 1887 and it opened for business in 1894. At the Manchester end, facilities were ready to accept the cargo vessels, with 200 acres of docks and 5 miles of quays. This proved attractive and a new commercial area was developed around them

The old and the new. In building the ship canal, the old Barton aqueduct had to be removed. This panoramic photograph shows the replacement swing aqueduct that still carries the Bridgewater Canal, with one of the many swing bridges in the background.

– Trafford Park. Many famous businesses moved in: The Co-operative Society had food warehouses and Kellogg's made cornflakes. It became a centre for innovation and some of the leading engineering companies, including Westinghouse, also moved in.

The Manchester Ship Canal was the last major canal undertaking completed in Britain, but it brings the story to a satisfactory conclusion. James Brindley's Bridgewater Canal is generally seen as marking the start of the country's enthusiasm for canals and its successor carried out the same basic function: linking the commercial heart of Manchester to the rest of the world. And Brindley would surely have been proud and amazed to find his canal swinging in mid-air. It demonstrated in dramatic fashion that the world of canals remained innovative to the end.

Further Reading

This is a select list of books that readers might find useful:

Anthony Burton, *The Canal Builders* (5th Ed.), 2015

Bertram Baxter, *Stone Blocks and Iron Rails*, 1966

Ruth Delaney, *Ireland's Inland Waterways*, 2004

T. K. Derry and Trevor I. Williams, *A Short History of Technology*, 1960

Harry Sinclair Drago, *Canal Days in America*, 1972

David Edwards-May, *Inland Waterways of France* (6th Ed.), 1991

Charles Hadfield, *British Canals* (8th Ed.), 1994

Charles Hadfield, *World Canals*, 1981

R. F. Leggett, *Canals of Canada*, 1972

Joseph Needham, *Science and Civilization in China, Vol. 4, Part 3*, 1986

L. T. C. Rolt, *From Sea to Sea* (2nd Ed.), 1994

Index